PRAISE FOR MARSH.

"Marshall's amazing adventures are distilled in a beautiful set of meditations on the natural world that will inspire you to renew both body and soul by following his example."
—Stephen Hanselman, co-author
of the international bestseller *The Daily Stoic*

*

"An athlete of astonishing grit...but there is also a
bit of Everyman in Marsh."
—Mark Burnett, Emmy-award-winning producer of
Survivor, The Voice, Shark Tank, and more

*

"One of America's greatest living adventurers
and expert without peer in human endurance."
—Christopher McDougall, author of *Born to Run*

*

"...what you have achieved...running the Badwater Quad, Badwater,
Western States and Leadville, and summiting the Seven Summits,
needed that gritty dogma and stubbornness that is in you."
—Ian Corless, *Runultra UK*

*

"The sport's [ultrarunning] figurehead in this country
is Marshall Ulrich."
—Florence Williams, *Outside* on-line

*

"Marshall's example is one that reminds us
all once again that endurance really is an attitude!"
—*Endurance Magazine*

MORE ABOUT MARSHALL ULRICH

Marshall Ulrich has appeared in *Running America, The Distance of Truth,* and *Running on the Sun* documentaries.

Ulrich is a member of the Colorado Running Hall of Fame, alongside Olympians Frank Shorter, Kara Goucher, and Jenny Simpson.

Ulrich has been a rich subject for scientist and authors studying and writing about endurance sports, including work by the University of Essex, exercise physiologists, cardiologists, and psychologists; and he's featured in *Born to Run* by Christopher McDougal, *To the Edge* by Kirk Johnson, and *Explorers of the Infinite* by Maria Coffey, and others.

~~~~~

Marshall Ulrich has been called:

The Endurance King
by *Outside* magazine

Zen Master of Extremes
In *The Distance of Truth* documentary

A Legend of the Trail
By *Trail Runner* magazine

Thermo Man
in *Stan Lee's Superhumans* TV series

BOTH FEET ON THE GROUND

REFLECTIONS FROM THE OUTSIDE

MARSHALL ULRICH

discover what *you're* made of
DNA Books

DNA Books, an imprint of:
Parker Hayden Media
5740 N. Carefree Circle, Suite 120-1
Colorado Springs, CO 80917

Art credits:
Cover design: Perry Gray
Cover photo: Rick Baraff

For my wife Heather,

my children Elaine, Taylor, and Alexandra,

and their spouses and children.

I love you!

INTRODUCTION

If you love a good story, I'm right there with you. Like so many children in the 1950s, I grew up reading and fantasizing about the world Jack London made for us, imagining myself as Buck the sled dog, overcoming neglect and harsh treatment, reclaiming my natural instincts, and leading a wild pack in the Yukon. Deft storytelling has probably whisked you off to distant places, too, made them real for you, raised your heart rate with tales of risk (look, a grizzly!), and given you a taste for adventure.

I wrote about my early fascination with London's classic *Call of the Wild* in my first book, a memoir. *Running on Empty* recounts my experiences as an ultramarathoner going distances that far exceed the standard 26.2 miles of a marathon. That's the sport I'm known for, if I'm known at all: a seemingly solitary, repetitive activity pursued mostly on roads and trails over hundreds or even thousands of miles. But people who knew more of my story prodded, "What about all the other 'crazy' stuff you've done? Why don't you write a book about *that?*"

They had a point. Mountain climbing and adventure racing have taken me from the world's densest jungles to the top of volcanos, on oceans and the tundra, and once on a trek in the hottest place on earth during the most blistering months on record. Many of my outdoor adventures are bizarre, funny, and possibly shocking, probably more interesting than my pursuit of running records. From the bottom of Death Valley to the top of Mount Everest, the cumulative impact of those experiences has been enormous: paradoxically, it's kept me sane. It's also given me respite from "real life" and made me especially grateful. Even more important to share, there's a purpose to all this that goes beyond what I've done or seen, or anything to do with me at all. It's a way of thinking about and dealing with the natural world and modern living, a perspective rooted in an old idea: *in wildness lies our preservation, the restoration of our best selves in body and in spirit.* I'm echoing Henry David Thoreau, but what do I mean? Breathing untainted air, testing ourselves in tough conditions, planting our feet and plunging our hands into the earth, sinking into a small or great body of water—all of these experiences connect us not only with a planet that needs our care, but also with some deeply grounded aspects of ourselves. London knew it! Thoreau and Muir were right! Although analysts' offices, self-help guides, and the rest of today's many aids have their place, one of the best forms of "therapy" can be summed up in one simple bit of advice: *Get out and stay out—as often and for as long as you can.*

I believe that there is a subtle magnetism in Nature,
which, if we unconsciously yield to it, will direct us aright.
—Henry David Thoreau

When I was a child, the outdoors were as much a part of my day as schoolrooms. Living on a dairy farm, my brother, sister, and I worked and played outside year-round, made forts of branches and boards, ran across grassy, manure-strewn fields, and tinkered with the tractor. We took care of the cattle in all kinds of weather. We chipped ice out of their drinking water when it froze, baled hay when the sun blazed, and made sure the cows were milked and fed every single day. Our responsibilities built muscle and mental strength, taught us to do what was necessary even when we didn't want to, even when it was uncomfortable and we'd rather have been doing anything else. This discipline on the farm foreshadowed and prepared me for my athletic pursuits as an adult, in which I've chosen to push my body toward its limits in harsh climates and on unforgiving terrain.

People ask me why I do these things. One answer is that this has served to show that humans—not just me, but all humans—are capable of much more than most of us imagine. We can take the heat. We can survive the cold. We can go farther and higher, and we can keep going long after we think we can't. Still, I have no illusions that extreme sports have made me Superman or Socrates; I'm neither indestructible nor especially wise. However, my interactions with the natural world, particularly immersion experiences where I've been stripped of all the extraneous *stuff* in my life, have prompted me to reconnect with what we all know on some level, with the instincts and practices most of us have lost or forgotten, with common sense, which isn't all that common anymore.

At its best, endurance leads to *discovery*, uncovering what we can learn by testing ourselves and demonstrating the vitality not only of dreaming, but also of doing something previously considered impossible. Exposing myself to the elements during severe tests of endurance has taught me to listen to my body about how much to eat, how often to rest, and how much discomfort I can take. It's shown me how intensely pleasurable the simplest things can be. It's also revealed the rewards of depending on others, the toll of deprivation, and the challenges related to the comforts and compulsions of contemporary life.

No matter what physical contest I've undertaken, the environment in which it's been held has made an important difference in my ability to endure it. In the middle of a 3,063-mile slog from San Francisco to New York City, the landscape—the bay water sloshing below the Golden Gate Bridge, for example, or the autumn color brightening the cold northeastern hills—all of it provided hours of distraction and the backdrop for daydreams. Some of the most joyous moments during that fifty-two-day outing happened when I got off the highway and ran on muddy, rutted roads. Nature can be equal parts beneficent and merciless. It can be a real mother, but it has saved my ass more than a few times.

Some years ago, Richard Louv coined the term "nature deficit disorder" to describe the negative effects of *depriving* ourselves of access to nature, of insulating ourselves within our constructed environments—our homes, offices, restaurants, theaters, museums, and so on. He described how city- and suburb-dwelling children's encounters with the natural world leaves them confused and disoriented. Trees and streams frighten rather than invite them to play and explore. His conclusion? When we don't give young people access to outdoor experiences like climbing over logs or building rock piles, chasing butterflies or collecting leaves, we get kids who can't abide the feel of mud in their hands, who are repulsed by anything that wiggles or flaps, who refuse to play with anything that isn't animated on an electronic device. They don't notice, can't relate to, and never learn the names of flora nor fauna. What's more, attention problems, anxiety, depression, and obesity plague them.[1]

Adults suffer from nature deficit disorder, too. Witness the rampant feelings of alienation and spiritual isolation, along with the rising use of antidepressants and anti-anxiety medications. The factors creating these problems are complex, but there's no question that simply getting up from the desk and going for a walk, or even looking up from the screen and out the window, helps. Imagine the profound benefits of doing more than that. Whereas we've known for some years now about the impact humans have on our environment, we're just now beginning to understand the impact particular environments have on humans—not just how pollution affects our breathing or how dwindling biodiversity might affect our food supply, but something else altogether: *What does it mean to live in a place increasingly devoid of nature?*

Ming Kuo, professor of natural resources and environmental science and psychology at the University of Illinois, has concluded that *access to nature* heavily influences our health and safety.

"Humans are evolved organisms and the environment is our habitat," Kuo said. "Now, as human societies become more urban, we as scientists are in a position to look at humans in much the same way that those who study animal behavior have looked at animals in the wild to see the effect of a changing habitat on this species."

Humans living in landscapes that lack trees or other natural features undergo patterns of social, psychological and physical break-down that are strikingly similar to those observed in other animals that have been deprived of their natural habitat...

Kuo and her colleagues have shown that these effects include decreased civility, less supervision of children outdoors, more illegal activity, more aggression, more property crime, more loitering, more graffiti and more litter.

"We might call some of that 'soiling the nest,' which is not healthy," she said. "No organisms do that when they're in good shape."

Certain psychological problems are also likely to appear more often in those lacking access to nature, she said.

"In our studies, people with less access to nature show relatively poor attention or cognitive function, poor management of major life issues, poor impulse control," she said.[2]

These people are like animals in an outmoded zoo, confined in cages, tearing out their fur, pacing urgently along the perimeter, throwing themselves repeatedly against the glass, smearing the place with their own waste, or sitting dejected in a corner.

It's strange that the boxes we've built for ourselves have become more comfortable and familiar than the natural world, which can seem foreign and dangerous. Our trappings are so much a part of our lives that when we don't have them, we hardly know what to do. Have you ever watched someone unravel when a phone is lost, a computer acts up, or the air conditioning shuts down? Our conveniences make life so much easier, don't they? So much safer and more predictable? I wonder. Old-timers would say they've made us soft. It's probably more accurate to say that we've become rigid, with our focus scoped down to tiny screens and our comfort zone narrowed to tight, climate-controlled, claustrophobic corridors. The more we cling to our conveniences, the crazier we get.

Remarkably, we can throw off the straitjackets of modernity any time we explore a wild place. We can realize and accept who we really are, trusting then testing our innate resilience, resourcefulness, and imagination. At a trail-running camp for wounded veterans (teamrwb.org), I saw several poignant examples of just how powerfully true this is. Held near Rocksprings, Texas, Camp Eagle uses physical and social activity to help vets deal with various troubles, from depression and anxiety to bodily injury and limb loss. It's a (mostly) controlled environment in which they experience and overcome additional challenges. On a rocky path, for instance, one fellow with a prosthetic leg worked out how to navigate a potentially destabilizing downhill. Another runner, still recovering from head trauma that had put her in a coma for three and a half months, learned to carefully think through foot placement on that same stretch. As coaches, we used the potent combination of smart risk-taking and immersion in an outdoor environment not just to boost confidence, but to help these men and women reclaim parts of themselves they thought they'd lost. It had value for them both as a literal exercise in ability and as a symbolic one. As my own experience had proven to me before, the work of Camp Eagle demonstrated how nature heals, how grounding it is to engage body and mind in adventure, even or especially when we think we're not fully capable.

Jack London's stories inspired me. Though I'm not the writer he was, I do have some tales and I can share my experiences, perhaps giving you some ideas for adventures of your own, possibly prodding you to be more daring. Of course, I've included some accounts of extreme distance running here—it's central to who I am as an athlete —but you'll also find plenty of other types of outdoorsy exploits. (Maybe this book can be a source of Vitamin N on its own; evidently, the brain doesn't distinguish between what's real and what's vividly imagined, so let's see if I can immerse you in what I've seen and done firsthand.)

This book, *Both Feet on the Ground: Reflections from the Outside,* shares stories of expeditions in such far-flung places as Borneo, Tibet, and South Africa, as well as my lifelong commitment to the land as a farmer in Colorado. In reading these reflections, you'll encounter some of what I have, along with some of the most useful findings and recommendations from other experts, all organized around themes of earth, air, fire, and water. By no coincidence, these parallel my experiences with farming, mountain climbing, desert running, and adventure racing. My hope is that you'll be inspired to find new ways of engaging with these natural elements yourself.

PART I

EARTH

HUMAN: NATURE

Be practical as well as generous in your ideals. Keep your eyes on the stars, but remember to keep your feet on the ground.
—Theodore Roosevelt, U.S. President, historian, naturalist, explorer, author, soldier

1

GROUNDING

Kids would press their palms against the big glass case where Mom and Dad displayed the candy at our old grocery store on the east side of Greeley, Colorado. A nickel would buy the biggest chocolate bar on the market, and if you didn't have that, a few pennies would do for a fistful of jaw breakers or a piece of bubble gum. My brother, Steve, and I were no different. At the end of the day after the customers had left, we searched under the cabinets in the store, and if we managed to score a little change, we'd sidle up to the East Side Market's display case, and buy some sweets, too.

The market provided our family with a modest small-town life, not so different from what you might see in a 1950s TV program like *The Andy Griffith Show*, with local characters and a bit of mischief. When Steve and I were three or four years old, we were shoveling snow and knocked out a few window panes for fun, then cleaned up the shards, thinking no one would notice. Dad caught on when the store temperature kept dropping, though, and we got a licking for it.

Shortly after that, in 1957, my mother decided that she and Dad needed to close the store and move us away from the "big city" of Greeley onto a farmstead in nearby Kersey. Not only would it keep us busy with chores, but it would also prevent us from getting into any worse trouble than our window caper. She believed it would teach us valuable lessons, the same lessons she had learned growing up in the beet fields of the Platte Valley. She wanted us to learn a solid work ethic. "Never put off for tomorrow what you can do today," she told us. Dad, a decorated veteran of World War II, had his own refrain: "If you want to succeed in life, discipline is the key." They were champions of hard work, believing that getting your hands dirty and staying close to the earth were the bedrock of a grounded, good life. Cultivating the land, caring for livestock, and making the most of everything we had were core skills they wanted to impart to their children because they believed it would make us strong, sensible, and industrious.

So off we went, and for the rest of my childhood, my family ran a small dairy farm in Kersey, Colorado. My life of leisure was over at five years old, as everyone had to work to keep the operation going. Up to eighty head of Holstein cattle on as many acres depended on the five of us—Mom, Dad, my brother, my sister Lonna, and me—to keep them in hay and milked regularly. As the herd moseyed around the corrals and pasture, swatted flies, and mooed at us and each other, we tended the fields. In the spring and summer, we grew alfalfa to dry and bale, then feed them in the winter.

We also cultivated about thirty acres of corn to cut and dry, which we'd supplement with more corn we got from the neighbors, to feed to the cows. In the fall, we harvested all of the ears, stems, and leaves, using a big corn chopper to nip the stalks a few inches from the ground and hack and mix everything into a silo (a big pit) to ferment and become silage. Dried kernels could also be ground up for a treat, and when we wanted to get the herd into the stanchions for milking, we'd fill the troughs and call to them: "Cow candy! Come getcher cow candy!" Not unlike those kids at the market, the Holsteins would press in to get at the sweet stuff—and take a double helping if we weren't looking.

For our own table, we tended a quarter-acre garden behind our small ranch-style house. Fresh vegetables piled up in the summer and fall, and Mom canned whatever she could to carry us through the cold months. We grew a pretty good year-round supply of food for everyone on the farm: Mom and Dad (Clara and Elmer) plus us three kids, the cows and a couple of pigs, and our dogs—Blackie the lab, Brownie the mutt, and (later) Puppy the border collie mix who helped herd the cattle into the milking catch pen. My parents didn't buy much from the store, except fresh fruit and a few staples. Mom made butter for us, using a hand-cranked separator to solidify the cream, as well as soap from lard and lye.

While Lonna worked mainly in the house with Mom, helping with unending chores of her own, Steve and I spent a lot of time together in the fields, spreading manure to fertilize the ground, and cutting, drying, baling, and loading hay. We milked a few cows by hand when they'd just had a calf, and we had machines to help us with the rest of them, usually fifty or sixty who were already producing milk—machines we cleaned and maintained regularly.

My dad; me and Steve; and Lonna and my mom (kneeling) celebrate
twin calves on our dairy farm in Kersey, CO in August 1959.

On the farm, there was always something that needed to be done. We worked before and after school and all day on Saturday. After church most Sunday mornings, the family took the afternoon for rest, which I usually spent drawing or reading on our back porch.

Though they were dedicated farmers, my parents never lost their entrepreneurial spirit, and Dad bought a business in the mid-1960s that he saw as a natural extension of both talents. He acquired the company because it was a chance to improve our quality of life, which tended to rise and fall with the seasons, as it does for all farmers. The price was right, too, because the owner needed to unload it in a hurry. A supplier for pet food companies, Weld County Bi-Products performed the free service of removing and disposing of dead livestock from local farms, ostensibly selling the raw meat to pet food manufacturers. The first company of its kind west of the Mississippi, WCBP's potential profits had been significant, but the owner had gotten greedy; instead of selling the meat for pet food, he'd peddled it at a premium for human consumption, which was a criminal act, and he'd gotten caught. So Dad snapped up WCBP for a bargain price, and the disgraced owner served a little jail time and moved on to other pursuits.

Our family rebuilt the business and its reputation with the local farms, the pet food manufacturers, and the public. In the beginning, Dad and a couple of employees drove the "dead truck," hauling fallen livestock—mostly dairy and stock cattle—back to the newly acquired plant in Greeley. There, skilled workers removed the hides, deboned the carcasses, and flash-froze the meat for sale to pet food manufacturers. They also loaded the bones, hooves, head, and entrails for delivery to a rendering facility and stored the hot feed from the stomach for us to use as fertilizer on our fields.

Sure, it was a grim family business, but it was an important service, not only to the farmers, but also to the community. Left to decompose naturally, large animals pose a hazard. They attract rats, snakes, flies, and other pests. They can contaminate the water supply. Disease may be spread by contact with the carcass. They smell, and can produce the toxins cadaverine and putrescine. Natural decomposition results in nearly three times the amount of greenhouse gas (methane) produced by rendering. So our business could be considered environmentally friendly, a kind of recycling, in that every part of the animal has a secondary purpose; we liked to say that we used everything but the moo. The bulk went to pet food, while the rendered by-products went to manufacturers of all kinds. Glue, solvents, anti-freeze, pharmaceuticals, film, crayons, soap, toothpaste, mouthwash, cosmetics, hair dye, nail polish, and shoe polish all contain rendered substances. Everyone from Fido and Fluffy to your first-grade teacher, your doctors, your mom and dad, and you benefit.

Just as I was finishing college, my dad asked me to help him run the family business. Although I'd studied fine arts and spent some time as an intern teaching elementary and high schoolers during my final two semesters at University of Northern Colorado, when I looked at the potential earnings of each career path, it was a relatively easy decision to make, and I told Dad I would help him expand to Fort Morgan, a nearby town. He already owned an empty building there, which he'd acquired as part of the WCBP purchase, and it needed to be rehabbed before I could open for business; the plumbing and electrical had been stripped, and all the windows smashed. I considered it a challenge to get things back in shape, and I looked forward to building my own branch of the business there. It would require my skills in design, fabrication, and construction, as well as the financial acumen I'd honed working with my dad at the Greeley plant when I was in high school as well as during weekends and breaks during college. I'd have to work with county, state, and federal agencies to get the permits and licenses we needed, and I'd need to start cultivating a clientele in an entirely new market for us.

This was the beginning of my adult life, and also my first adult reckoning with Death. Not the lowercase death of livestock or people you read about in the newspaper, but the kind that completely redefines the word for you because it is frightening and so damned personal. The kind that reminds you of your own mortality, of how little control you have over the length of your own life.

It started happily enough: The day after my fiancée Jean Schmid and I graduated from college, we got married, and two days later moved to Fort Morgan to establish the family business there. Jean started law school a year later while I followed in Dad's footsteps, driving the "dead truck" myself and building up a clientele. Over the next few years, I was able to hire more and more employees, and we gained traction, eventually outpacing the three other rendering businesses in the area. Our secret? Fort Morgan Pet Foods went a little further, providing service 24/7 long before that phrase caught on, regardless of weather. I drove into livestock pens so farmers wouldn't have to move dead animals themselves (cattle can weigh up to twenty-four hundred pounds), and I established routes so that folks with the larger feedlots wouldn't have to call me—I just showed up every day to see if they needed my help. Half-joking, I started calling myself a "used-cow dealer."

By the time the business really started to take off, Jean was finishing up her Juris Doctor degree. She was also pregnant, and when she sat for the bar exam, she was eight months along. As expected, she passed the bar on her first try, and within a month, she gave birth to our baby girl. Holding Elaine in my arms, standing next to Jean's hospital bed, I couldn't imagine life would ever be better than this.

We bought our first house together, a twenty-two-hundred-square-foot split level on Paynter Place in Morgan Heights, which I enjoyed outfitting with a solar heating system I devised myself. Everywhere I turned, I thought I had things fixed up and running smoothly; at home and in business, my hard work was paying off.

Then, just as Elaine was learning to walk, we were blindsided by the news that Jean had invasive breast cancer. Her doctor recommended immediate surgery, and Jean underwent a double mastectomy within days of this diagnosis. She started chemotherapy less than a week later.

My wife, a petite, health-conscious spitfire of a woman, couldn't understand *why* she had this disease. She didn't smoke or drink. She exercised. She had no family history of breast cancer. *What*, Jean wondered, *have I done to bring this on myself?* There was no answer to that question, and all I could do to comfort her was to empathize. *I'd be mad, too, if it was me.*

Jean bounced back for a while, but the cancer returned, and she was forced to leave her law practice. In dark echoes of my happiest moments, there were many times that I held Elaine in my arms by Jean's hospital bed. As the disease progressed, it overtook her brain and crossed her eyes, then metastasized to her lungs, bones, and liver. Less than a year after her surgery, Jean's life was over. I was thirty years old, and Elaine had just turned three.

This painful loss scarred me. It also gave me a powerful conviction and a new passion: running. Not only did the running control my stress-related high blood pressure, but it allowed me to escape and find a peace within myself that the everyday world couldn't provide. At first, I sprinted around our home town of Fort Morgan, Colorado, pushing myself as hard as I could, as often as I could. Nearly every morning I covered about five or six miles, regularly incorporating what today's athletes know as hill repeats. I ran up and down challenging inclines over and over again, having no idea that this was a training technique; it was just a hilly landscape, and that's what I did to blow off steam. At that stage of life, I'd never before exerted myself for any purpose other than work (or, as a child, play), so it didn't occur to me to keep track of my mileage or, for that matter, what races I entered. The whole point of running, in my mind, was to bust loose, to break away, to give myself a chance to grieve for Jean in private, to escape the grim progression of her illness.

Occasionally, I picked up a copy of *Runner's World*, but what I read there seemed far removed from my life. The gear reviews and the training advice were foreign; the amount of advertisements for running fashion and fitness trends mind-boggling. For me, running was about keeping my sanity, quieting the noise in my head. There was too much else going on to be bothered with comparing the latest shoes or finding the best way to strengthen my quads.

Whenever Jean and I ventured into Denver, usually for medical appointments, we saw nearby Mount Evans, as it's one of the mountain peaks that dominates the western skyline of the Great Plains, jutting out of the Front Range of the Rocky Mountains. I'd heard about a 14.5-mile race there, the Mount Evans Ascent, billed as "America's Highest Road Race." It has been described, perhaps hyperbolically, as "not so much a race as an ordeal."[1] The distance seemed within reach for me, a little more than double my usual six-mile outings, and the mountain foot race sounded like a worthy challenge.

The race begins at Echo Lake, 10,600 feet above sea level, and from there goes up almost four thousand vertical feet, rising above treeline within four miles of the start and continuing to the finish line at the peak of the mountain at 14,264 feet. Back then, all I knew was that I wanted to do it, although in retrospect I realize that, as Jean's health worsened, I felt that I needed to prove and punish myself. So I ran a little farther sometimes and dug a little deeper as I looked forward to race day.

Arriving that morning, thinking I really had no business being there, I was exhilarated anyway. Nearly a thousand people had entered and were crowding toward the starting line. Clean, crisp, cold air filled my nostrils. About three miles up the road, we ran through a bristle-cone forest of bent and twisted trees, thousands of years old, and I took comfort in the fact that they had survived and they continued to persevere. For the first time, I felt very small and humbled by my surroundings, and paradoxically, this made it easier to keep running up, up, up.

Rising in elevation, I was amazed by the plowed snow on the side of the road, sometimes reaching twelve feet deep, slow to melt, and some of which I knew would linger through the summer. Then came a slightly flat and downhill section five miles from the top and a run down to Summit Lake where the peak of Mount Evans loomed above. This is a paved road, but somehow, marmots burrow underneath it, and as I ran I saw them pop their heads out from the middle of the road as if to check us out and cheer us on. At what seemed to be a painstakingly slow pace, I continued up the ever-increasing switch-backs and steep grades to the finish where I knew Jean would be wait-ing. When I reached the top after about two-and-a-half hours, I celebrated with her, and although she was in the midst of a second round of strength-sapping chemotherapy, Jean jumped up and down in her excitement for me. I hugged and kissed her, and we celebrated my seemingly impossible accomplishment together. We took home the finisher's trophy, a chunk of rock awarded to men and women who finish in under 2:40 and 3:00 respectively, and we displayed it on our bedside table.

This memory of her—vibrant, victorious, happy for me, strong despite the horrible disease she was fighting—is the last one I have of her at a race with me, and one that comes to mind when I look into Elaine's eyes, so much like her mother's and now a mother herself—or when I'm in a tough situation and need to marshal strength to carry on. My wife was a wonder.

Elaine and Jean.

Jean survived six more months after that mountaintop moment. As she became more ill, I continued to run, tackling hills, developing a feel for mountain trails, and seeking more difficult races. Three months before the cancer took Jean's life in 1981, I ran up Pikes Peak for the first time, completing the Ascent of 7,815 feet in the half-marathon distance of 13.32 miles, arriving at the top alone, feeling a strange mix of emotions: a thundering guilt that my wife was at home, suffering, along with elation and a stubborn sense of self-preservation. *Should I even be here? Why am I healthy, and she is not? Am I one selfish S.O.B., or what?*

After Jean died, I became single-minded about kicking dust in Death's face and exhausting myself in pursuit of relief from my survivor's guilt. I've completed the official Pikes Peak Marathon, double the distance of my first ascent, nine times over the years since then. My memoir, *Running on Empty,* is largely about the ripple effects of Jean's death, how my unresolved pain drove me not only to run farther, to punish myself, but also to seek adventure at every turn—to confront my fears and to pursue my dreams. As an endurance athlete with tens of thousands of miles now behind me, I've devoted myself to testing the human body, going beyond previously perceived limits.

If I want to be melodramatic, I can say that I've thumbed my nose at Death. More simply, I can affirm, *I'm alive.*

The father of three children—Elaine, Taylor, and Ali—I am also a grandfather, and I've become a happy husband once again. My wife Heather has helped me heal, though I admit I am still learning. I'm still farming on land that Dad, Lonna, Steve, and I bought together in the 1980s ("ELMS Farms" stands for Elmer, Lonna, Marshall, and Steven), where we grow pinto beans, field corn, and wheat on over one thousand acres. When conditions are right and the crops are good, we produce a hundred and fifty thousand to two hundred thousand bushels of corn each year. Imagine a semi load, a forty- to fifty-foot trailer, and know that it holds twelve hundred to thirteen hundred bushels. Then picture 120 to 175 semis filled with corn, and you get a sense of the volume we produce.

Machines do most of the work, but I still help with the harvest and load out the corn. They don't really need me there; I do it because I like it. I enjoy working in the fresh air, seeing the people from year to year. I like the earthy humor of farmers and agricultural workers, and I love to eat with them in diners with simple menus. Besides, these folks are so grounded; we share common respect for space, distance, growth, and loss. They, like me, have made their peace with the elements, the seasons, the discipline, the disappointments, the quiet elation you can feel when you sway in concert with the rhythms of nature.

WHEN I CONSIDER how most children spend their time today, I'm struck by the gulf between their experiences and my own, but I'm hardly the first person to consider the ramifications of it. Richard Louv has observed, "An indoor (or backseat) childhood does reduce some dangers to children; but other risks are heightened, including risks to physical and psychological health, risk to children's concept and perception of community, risk to self-confidence, and the ability to discern true danger." All that is decidedly true, and, because of my upbringing, I think about some of the other losses sustained by detachment from the natural world, particularly farms. Ask most kids where their food comes from, and they will say things like, "We get ours from the refrigerator," or "We buy it at the supermarket." Many don't give a thought to what happens before food lands on their plates, much less before it goes to market.

When celebrity chef Jamie Oliver polled some high schoolers, he found that, given a multiple choice food quiz using pictures of a cow, an ear of corn, and a sunflower, many thought butter comes from corn. Then he asked about sausages: are they made from a cow, a dachshund, or corn dogs? For corn dogs, he actually showed them a picture of cattails, the wetland plant with a hot-dog shaped flower. Most chose the "corn dog plant," citing it as the source for sausages.

When I first read about this, I had to let that sink in: they believed corn dogs bloom at the end of a stalk and concluded, *That's where sausage comes from.* There was more: many didn't know what almonds are, much less that nuts grow on trees, and they reckoned that chocolate comes from a chocolate lake![2] A study of 27,500 five- to sixteen-year-olds in the United Kingdom showed that a third of the children thought that cheese comes from plants instead of cows' milk, and a fifth of them didn't know bacon comes from pigs. About a third of the five- to eight-year-olds thought that pasta and bread are made from meat.[3] A tenth of the young people in one survey thought eggs came from wheat instead of chickens...no "yolk."

Food surveys conducted in other countries reveal similar results. And, so we're clear, it's not only among the children: U.S. consumer research conducted in 2011 revealed that 72 percent of the adults surveyed knew next to nothing about farming and ranching.[4] Not surprising, in that few people live on farms, and fewer still visit them to find out how their food is produced.

Let's call this specific kind of nature deficit disorder a "food fugue": *denial of or plain disregard for the source of our food.* Just as Robert Louv described problems related to a lack of access to nature—confusion in the outdoors, intolerance of dirt, dependence on electronic devices for entertainment, irrational fear of wild animals and insects, plus the tagalong issues of short attention spans, anxiety, depression, and obesity—I can point out the problems with food fugue. Consider these: control issues, like obsessive worry about eating the "right" things or intense fear of eating the "wrong" things; mindlessly consuming too much food; buying into food marketing gimmicks; dependence on processed and fast food; and an absence of basic cooking skills, including such simple things as knowing when fruit is ripe, the names of vegetables, or how to prepare a hot meal without a microwave oven.

Why do we allow ourselves to become so detached and disengaged? Why do we choose to shut out the natural world, adapting to an artificial habitat, dulling our instincts, and becoming apathetic about the most basic element of our survival: food? It's pretty simple, I think. Being disconnected from nature, including what we eat, can make us feel quite *comfortable*. It can shield us from dirt, from sweat and hard work, and from considering how our choices reflect our values and affect the world around us. It can give us our steak without having to confront the realities of the slaughterhouse. It can deliver us a year-round supply of our favorite flavors without concern for how consuming them expands our carbon footprint.

Now, I invite you to be uncomfortable. You may find, as I have, that temporary, voluntary discomfort can yield disproportionate rewards. A simple example: if you are a backyard gardener, you know how satisfying a just-picked tomato can taste, the flavor enhanced not only by its freshness but by your history with its vine. You spent time digging, hauling, watering, weeding, fertilizing. You probably swatted a few bugs. You stuck your hands in the soil, got them dirty, and tended the vine, pruning occasionally by pinching off shoots that sprouted where they shouldn't, and then smelled the tomato essence on your fingers; a seedling grew into a plant which bore fruit that you then put on your dinner table. You coaxed the miraculous out of the mundane, and you savored it. *That* is what connecting with nature can give you.

It's one of the reasons I still grow food, even if it's on a massive scale. There's value in planting, tending, waiting, and harvesting. Corn takes about four months from the time you push the seed into the soil until you're harvesting ears from the stalk, so you have to be patient and vigilant. The plants need to be spaced right, and they need consistent watering and protection from pests like raccoons, deer, beetles, corn borers, cutworms, and root aphids. Once sweet corn is mature, there's simply nothing like grabbing an ear off the stalk and then running as fast as you can, shucking as you go, so that by the time you get to the house you can drop it right into the pot. When corn is plucked fresh and plunged into boiling water before there's time for the sweet-tasting sugars to start converting to starches, the taste is transcendent. Because of my upbringing, I grieve for those who never do this or anything like it—never pick a berry off a bush, never grow a sunflower, never tend a garden of their own. Truly, no video game can replace it. Watching it on TV doesn't remotely give you the same thrill. Having food available to you with no effort, tidy and packaged and seemingly perfect, may spare you a chore (months of chores!), but it takes away something you may never even be able to name.

Will Allen, a former pro basketball player who works with youth at his urban farm in Milwaukee, offers this explanation: "It's way more than just putting a plant in the ground," Allen says. "It's about learning some life skills in terms of how to take care of yourself, how to take care of your body, how to be able to work in this environment. It's about learning how to eat healthy, to be able to build things by doing something hands-on.... Kids that come in here, they're wired and they're bouncing off the walls. But as soon as I put some soil in their hands, they just calm down," Allen says. "There's something very spiritual about touching the soil."[5]

Working the land goes beyond metaphor and analogy; it teaches you more than the rewards of labor, the impermanence of seasons, the progression of time. You come to *know* the soil, the texture and density of it, the smell and the feel and the even the taste of it. You become more aware of the weather, not just how it dictates what to wear, but how it affects the growth of plants, the color and health of the leaves, the abundance or lack of fruit. You discover your own strength and a kind of ingenuity born of the need to extract a cantankerous root or move a heavy load of dirt. You learn which insects are beneficial and which bring disease. You don't "master" the land, nature, the environment. You are part of it.

2

SUSTENANCE

ONE OF THE perks of being an extreme endurance athlete is that you become an expert in the second-most pleasurable human activity: eating. Consuming enough food to successfully train for and compete in multi-day sports requires that you become a student of sustenance, a connoisseur of calories, a bona-fide authority in the art of chowing down. Sustaining physical exertion any longer than about an hour demands that you replenish energy stores, and that you do it wisely, or else you risk hitting the wall (bonking) or enduring gut pain, headache, diarrhea, vomiting, and worse. And when we're talking about continuing on for much longer than that—days or weeks or months—eating becomes a serious mental and physical discipline. You can learn a great deal by pushing yourself to the limits, including exactly what and when you need to eat so you can keep on going.

For the last three decades, I've been doing exactly that. In my thirties, I took up ultrarunning and set records in races that lasted twenty-four hours or more; in my forties, I began adventure racing with other elite athletes, competing in far-flung locales on courses of three hundred to five hundred miles that took up to ten days to complete; in my fifties, I fulfilled a lifelong dream of climbing Mount Everest and went on to reach the summits of the tallest mountains on all seven continents, and all but one took two to six weeks. The toughest test of them all came when I was fifty-seven years old and completed the equivalent of two marathons and a 10K every day for nearly two months straight by running from San Francisco to New York City.

Those experiences have given me an intimate understanding and appreciation of a few things: terrain—the more than ninety thousand miles of earth that has passed under my feet, in all kinds of landscapes and altitudes and weather—and the human capacity to exceed perceived limits. With each new outing, I marvel at the variety of our natural environments, as well as how the body can adapt and respond to just about anything we ask of it. Going beyond my own imagined boundaries—physical, emotional, psychological, and spiritual—has taught me about myself, certainly, but it has also taught me a great deal about human potential, determination, discipline, and the value of finishing whatever you start.

Besides that, of course, I know how to eat.

Listen to your body. We are each an experiment of one.
—George Sheehan

THROUGH THE YEARS, I've learned what works for me, and I recognize with respect that it doesn't necessarily work for everyone. Not every runner will relish roadside chili con carne during a 135-mile race, and certainly not everyone who reads this book will want to run sixty-plus miles and consume nine thousand or more calories per day, or ascend to the death zone on Mount Everest and snack on smoked pig rinds. Again, I recognize that what my body needs or craves, or what my gut can process and turn into fuel for the long haul, or what I deem delicious or worthy or "good" isn't the de facto recommended human diet. Genetics and predispositions make dietary choices highly individual, as do specific health issues, activity level, and personal ethics.

However, I have also learned some universal truths. For instance, spending time outdoors, particularly when you're exerting yourself, can fully reacquaint you with your senses. Doing so over several days can heighten those senses and help you regain forgotten instincts and even re-integrate with a natural environment, recognizing that you are not separate from nature but instead a part of it. Yet modern Americans, if they exercise at all, tend to exercise indoors, in a gym. Most don't walk to work or school; they travel inside a vehicle. Most also drive to acquire food from a supermarket or restaurant instead of walking into their backyard or to a local farm or farmers' market, and then they eat it in the car, at the kitchen table, or a break room. Most sleep in bedrooms lit with electronic devices and LCD screens. All of these habits serve to shut down our instincts—they can definitely blunt mine—and I believe this is a primary source of people's intense confusion, and in some cases obsession, with eating the "right" foods.

Disconnection from and distrust of our instincts leaves us vulnerable to marketing gimmicks. *Why is knowing what food to buy so complicated for consumers?* In addition, it makes the "rules" of eating fuzzy. *Why is this most basic of human acts so fraught?* And it can lead to anger and defensiveness. *Why do so many people who adhere to a prescribed diet become rigid and obsessive?*

As with most big questions, nature provides some clues.

Have you ever heard that crows collect and hoard shiny things? Well they don't, actually. At least, wild crows don't. This idea that they can't resist a bit of bling is probably based on what *captive* birds do. Young corvids that are hand-raised from the time they are chicks will develop an affinity for keys, coins, jewelry, and so on—the common trappings of the human home. But an uncaged, unmolested crow will grow up pecking at and picking up acorns and twigs and rocks and other things they find in nature. They will also tuck away a cache of food, but they won't swoop into your car or living room to snatch, then hoard, pretty little trinkets. That is a myth. The only crows that are unable to resist bright, shiny objects are those with a warped sense of who they are.

Generally, crows are very smart, but they aren't smart enough to overcome the allure of useless junk if they have been conditioned to want it. Evidently, neither are most humans.

Influences that counter our own natural instincts surround us in affluent, industrialized countries. Food packaging. Commercials.

Nutritional content labels. Social media. Also culture, values, and social class, along with personal taste and the properties of a food itself —all of these serve to condition us just as the captive crow has been conditioned, which is to say that we are often manipulated into thinking we want things we don't need.

We're susceptible to manipulation through our emotions, primarily. Fear is a powerful motivator, and the debate about genetically modified organisms (GMO) offers clear examples of how fear can be used to sway the public. First, consider the rhetoric. Who wants to eat something called "Frankenfood"? In the United States, most corn, soy, canola, and sugar beets are genetically engineered, and all of these are common ingredients in processed foods, so like it or not, you are probably eating some of these little "monsters" already. But are they really so scary? Although only 37 percent of the American public believe GMOs are okay to consume, 88 percent of the members of the American Association for the Advancement of Science insist GMOs are safe to eat.[1] That's a pretty big gap between public and scientific opinion.

Like most questions about the merits of certain foods, this one is complex, however. It's not settled strictly by science. Some like to paint it as a David and Goliath scenario, with food giants wanting to protect their GMOs so they can make money, money, money, and grass-roots crunchy granola types trying to defend the health of the nation. That's not quite right. The truth is, most everyone is trying to turn a profit. Here are the facts as I understand them:

Pro-GMO

- Americans have been eating GMO foods for nearly two decades and there's no proof that they are harmful.
- The use of genetically modified seed has helped farmers decrease the use of pesticides on crops.
- GMOs have the potential to decrease carcinogens in the foods we eat.
- GMOs have greatly increased yields per acre, reducing the amount of land it takes to grow food. They help us to more efficiently feed the world.

- GMOs produce plants that are more drought-resistant, helping us to combat larger issues, like global warming.

No-GMO

- No studies have been completed to determine the effects of consuming genetically engineered ingredients over a person's lifetime. Some animal studies indicate that GMO foods may adversely affect the immune system, liver, and kidneys.
- Although we have reduced use of insecticides, we have increased use of herbicides by about ten times, leading to the growth of resistant "super-weeds," which may prompt development of new GMOs along with new herbicides. Opponents say this is no solution at all, and may create even worse problems to solve. Although GMOs may reduce pesticides overall, it may ultimately increase the amount of herbicides that wind up in our food.

No matter what you think about all of this, you should know that one striking result of the public debate about it is new *marketing strategies* designed to get you to buy stuff: foods labeled "organic" that barely satisfy the criteria and the same old products rolled out under the "non-GMO" banner, not to mention all the new products attempting to capitalize on the public's worries and whims. Until we can determine, conclusively, the net effects of GMOs upon people and the planet, every individual's opinion about this remains only that: an opinion.

Right now, 92 percent of Americans believe their food should be labeled GMO if it contains any genetically engineered ingredients. Agribusiness is pushing back, hard, opposing the myriad bills that are being introduced to states' legislatures. Both sides are putting major financial resources into the fight:

Labeling is backed by its own special interests, chiefly the organic and natural foods industries, which would presumably see their market share increase if consumers suddenly confronted GMO labels on grocery shelves. Major financial backers of labeling include organic-food manufacturers such as Amy's Kitchen and Nature's Path, the organic-soap company Dr. Bronner's, and the dietary-supplement marketer and vaccination critic Joseph Mercola. The campaign for labeling isn't purely activist-driven—it's a coordinated national effort on the part of groups like the Center for Food Safety and Just Label It, a project of the Environmental Working Group. The national groups aid local activists with resources and strategy.[2]

Which begs the question, "What does "organic" mean?" According to the U.S. Department of Agriculture, "Overall, organic operations must demonstrate that they are protecting natural resources, conserving biodiversity, and using only approved substances." It endorses "levels" of organic-ness, based mainly on those approved substances and some practices that "certify" a food as organic, meaning some foods can be labeled "100 percent organic," some "organic," and some "made with organic." In other words, *organic* means one thing to the backyard gardener, who shuns chemical pest controls and fertilizers, and something else entirely to the food conglomerate that is trying to capture market share.

This GMO versus organic argument exemplifies the battle constantly waged for consumer dollars, for your dollars. You are continually presented with bright, shiny objects—new products with exciting promises of this or that health benefit, or frightening threats of this or that health scare—that have nothing to do with you making good food choices. (By the way, did you know that you can now buy gluten-free bacon? It's true! Of course, bacon never contained gluten, but that's beside the point. Caw caw, little crow.) It has everything to do with getting as much of your money as possible, spent on packaged, processed food: cereal ("Made with whole grains!"), chips ("Less fat!"), frozen dinners ("All natural!"), and the rest.

We don't have to respond like Pavlov's dogs, however, salivating every time they ring the bell. We can wise up to these gimmicks and realize that, for the most part, it is all just noise, the cacophony of the marketplace, carnival barkers trying to get our attention.

Then how do you figure out what is actually good for you? You can't go by the latest nutrition advice in your social media feed, or even the "hot new discoveries" in science journals. In his book *Food Rules,* Michael Pollan stresses that "nutrition science is, to put it charitably, a very *young* science." Basically, everything we think we know is up for debate. Yet, he says, there are two indisputable facts:

1) People who eat the usual Western diet of high-calorie processed foods, fat, sugar, and refined grains, and nearly no vegetables, predictably develop obesity, type 2 diabetes, cardiovascular disease, and cancer; and

2) Practically any other diet is better than that. Populations in other parts of the earth, who eat differently than Westerners do, typically don't get these so-called Western diseases. The range of superior diets is wide:

> These diets run the gamut from ones very high in fat (the Inuit in Greenland subsist largely on seal blubber) to ones high in carbohydrate (Central American Indians subsist largely on maize and beans) to ones very high in protein (Masai tribesmen in Africa subsist chiefly on cattle blood, meat, and milk), to cite three rather extreme examples.... What this suggests is that **there is no single ideal human diet but that the human omnivore is exquisitely adapted to a wide range of different foods and a variety of different diets.**[3]
> [Emphasis added.]

After extensive journalistic investigation, Pollan arrives at some simple conclusions: If we want to be responsible consumers—making choices that both support our health and a sustainable system of food production—then we need to return to eating in a way that *depends more on nature* and less on manufacturing (and, by implication, marketing). Or as he puts it, "Eat food. Mostly plants. Not too much." As often as possible, forego processed foods and for goodness' sake, forget dieting. Instead, eat slower and enjoy your food. If, from time to time, you want a hoagie or a Twinkie or even a whole loaf of white bread, have at it. But if you also want to avoid the most common "lifestyle diseases," follow Pollan's advice: eat real food, mostly plants, in reasonable quantities. Avoiding disease is one thing. Maximizing performance is another. They aren't mutually exclusive, but they do have different demands, so let's take a look at that for a minute.

Although I don't often make a fuss about other people's choices, I'm not above kicking over a hornet's nest just for the hell of it. I've had a laugh or two by poking fun at one of the most accomplished ultrarunners of all time, Scott Jurek, by suggesting that he might be an even more super superman if he'd have a bite of steak every once in a while. (Scott eats a vegan diet and, at one time, had completed the fastest known time on the more than two-thousand -mile Appalachian Trail.) When I did this, people chastised and lectured me, called me names, impugned my reputation and intentions, and rushed to defend Scott's honor. It's to be expected; diets can be controversial, and I suspect nowhere does the discussion get more heated than in the athletic community. From what I've seen, beliefs and practices verge on religious devotion. Whenever I've posted something on my blog or social media about the merits of eating meat, the arguments are immediate and lengthy.

Online and off, people with choices about what to eat debate nearly constantly about what we "should" eat. Have you seen anything similar in your own life? Uncle George decides he's never having bread again and starts glaring at the stuffing on the table for Thanksgiving, and suddenly it turns into a family feud, with Cousin Nancy pronouncing gluten-free diets a sham and Cousin Ned feeling deeply offended because he made the dish. How dare anyone voice an opinion! Meanwhile, Aunt June suffers quietly, wondering if Ned would be so defensive if he knew about her recent diagnosis of Celiac's disease.

The blood-type diet. Atkins. South Beach. Mediterranean. Banting. Paleo, primal, primitive. Gluten-free. Vegetarian, vegan, fruitarian. *Potato, potah-toe, tomato, tomah-toe. Let's call the whole thing off.* Diets are just one more way of either obsessing over what you put into your mouth or abdicating all decisions to some questionable authority.

Yet anyone who asserts that they have some kind of silver bullet is full of it. "I have the best diet that produces the best results for the best of everything in your life.... Just do this *one thing* and you'll be the best, too!" Don't eat that! Eat this! Take this supplement! Try this gel! I say no. No to all of it, at least as a panacea or some kind of performance "secret." Indeed, what sets apart the superstars, the Jureks and achievers in a multitude of other endeavors, isn't "one thing." It's not vegan or vegetarian or Paleo or primal—performance is more about training and talent, hard work, and good genes. That ain't news, and it ain't sexy, I know. But it's the truth.

My own opinions on the matter come from being both a farmer and an athlete, having personally tested the benefits and limitations of various eating plans (yes, I was a vegetarian for a couple of years).

Harvesting corn and loading it into storage bins for later sale on our farm ground near Yuma, CO in 2017.

They come from talking with other athletes, nutritionists, and scientists who study the effects of extreme sport on the biological processes of the human body. They are also informed by a key idea: separating ourselves from nature is a mistake with inestimable costs, and connecting with nature—particularly our own nature, both collectively and as individuals—reintroduces us to core truths and a grounded wisdom for a more fulfilling and, dare I say, *wholesome* life. Meaning: wholesome as conducive to mental and physical health, and also as conducive to moral well-being. This morality, as it relates to food, is dictated by your own beliefs about it, and those beliefs may be religious or secular. So let me be clear, because it seems as if every time I engage in a discussion about this, people misunderstand.

What I AM NOT saying:

1. You must eat meat to be healthy.
2. Athletes must eat animal protein and fat to perform well.
3. I am an expert on what everyone else's body needs.
4. You must compromise your values to succeed in sport.
5. Factory farming is a humane, acceptable way of producing food.

What I AM saying (surprise!):

1. *People with average exercise habits can get sufficient protein and calories from a strictly plant-based diet (i.e., vegan or vegetarian).* I do not have average exercise habits, and have determined that eating only plant-based foods doesn't work for me. Based on conversations with lots of long-distance runners, I don't believe it works so well for others, either. Ted Corbitt, called "the father of ultrarunning" and one of the founders and architects of the sport, once told me about his relatively brief time as a vegetarian. He eliminated meat from his diet for a few years in his forties, but then developed anemia, and his doctor insisted he reintroduce animal protein. When he did, problem solved. Not incidentally, Ted was notable not only for his early success in running as an Olympic athlete and as a race organizer, but for his feats when competing in the masters' category. At age eight-three, he walked 303 miles in a six-day race, covering just over fifty miles a day. He lived to the age of eighty-eight.) I've spoken with others who've had similar experiences and, as I mentioned earlier, gave vegetarianism a try for a while myself before I started tackling ultra distances. Either I'm not good at it, or it's not good for me; regardless, I returned to eating meat.

In the United States, the recommended daily consumption of protein is forty-six and fifty-six grams per day for women and men, respectively, over nineteen years of age.[4] Most Americans have no trouble meeting this amount and, in fact, most eat twice as much. For reference, five egg whites or a palm-sized chicken breast yields twenty grams of protein. So does a serving of Greek yogurt or a plateful of kidney beans. Or about seven cups of kale.)

Studies have shown that eating a high-protein diet may be

beneficial for the heart, as long as the protein comes from a healthy source, such as green leafy vegetables[5] instead of, say, chile verde. In talking with "normal" athletes, I generally recommend a diet of 60 percent carbohydrates, 20 percent fat, and 20 percent protein—with a good mix of meat and plant-based sources for all of these. Variety is not only the spice of life, but it is also the best way to make sure you're eating well.

2. Animal proteins and fats have greater caloric density and are more readily and rapidly used by our bodies than proteins in plants. For me, eating meat helps ensure adequate energy for multiday events and can prevent problems like muscle wasting (catabolic breakdown), which happens when you don't get enough protein. The boon to athletes of meat is the sheer quantity of calories and grams of protein that it delivers in each bite. This is also why those with a sedentary lifestyle are wise to limit it or eliminate it altogether. For most people, the "best" diet can include some lean protein from animals but relies mostly on plants for well-rounded nutrition: Limiting animal protein (particularly because of its casein content, which plants don't have) intake may reduce risk of cancer, according to research explored in T. Colin Campbell's book, *The China Study.*

3. Our digestive systems are equipped to use whatever we put in our mouths (within reason) as fuel. We are lucky evolution has made us omnivores. Scientists debate whether or not we're biological omnivores, citing the construction of our jaw, hands, and gut, among other things, but it is plainly obvious that humans are, at the very least, behavioral omnivores, meaning that we can choose to eat nearly anything. Humans across the planet survive on insects and grasses, nuts and berries, cultivated crops and livestock, wild game. You name it, and someone is probably eating it.

Clearly, this has evolutionary benefits—we're less likely to starve if one of our food sources dries up—but it also has some drawbacks for modern humans. Paradoxically, those drawbacks are at odds: 1) we have the ability to become overwhelmed by our choices and feel helpless to make the "right" ones, 2) we have an equal ability to stop thinking about our choices at all, and then feel as if we have no responsibility for them, and 3) we can become so fervent in our choices that we make ourselves tense with a kind of moral rigidity. As it turns out, you can actually care too much about what you eat. You can obsess about it, record it, plan it, prepare it, analyze it. You can become so unbending that any indulgences feel like sin, any transgressions result in emotional self-flagellation, and others' choices are subject to your judgmental criticism. Dr. Steven Bratman coined a term for this in 1996, *orthorexia nervosa,* which is "fixation on righteous eating."

Orthorexia starts out as an innocent attempt to eat more healthfully, but orthorexics become fixated on food quality and purity. They become consumed with what and how much to eat, and how to deal with "slip-ups." An iron-clad will is needed to maintain this rigid eating style. Every day is a chance to eat right, be "good," rise above others in dietary prowess, and self-punish if temptation wins (usually through stricter eating, fasts and exercise). Self-esteem becomes wrapped up in the purity of orthorexics' diet and they sometimes feel superior to others, especially in regard to food intake.

Eventually food choices become so restrictive, in both variety and calories, that health suffers—an ironic twist for a person so completely dedicated to healthy eating. Eventually, the obsession with healthy eating can crowd out other activities and interests, impair relationships, and become physically dangerous.[6]

As the Buddha counseled, wisdom lies in the middle way. What might happen if we routinely considered the impact—personally, ethically, and ecologically—of our food choices, and we also allowed ourselves to indulge from time to time? What if we took a moment every now and again to delight in the fact that we have choices at all?

What I eat is based entirely on listening to my body and letting it direct me to foods that will sustain me. During long (five- to fifty-day) endurance events, those foods are different from my day-to-day diet, and each sport demands something different. On adventure-racing teams, we sometimes went for days with water but no food, burning body fat and doing well. During my run across the U.S., I needed to consume upward of nine thousand calories a day, and it was as much a matter of finding something—anything—that was palatable while I was in pain, as it was of ensuring adequate calories.

One of my jobs during my 2008 run across America was to consume enough calories to keep me moving.

During that effort, I lost a grand total of four pounds, so I'm pretty sure I was doing something right. My body changed, however: my calf muscles shrank, my quads and glutes were pretty well jacked, and my upper body muscles (from carrying bottles of liquid) had gotten larger and firmer, too.

Normally, I have a simple, balanced diet with limited fats, more protein than the minimum recommended daily allowance, and limited carbs. During endurance events, it can be kind of bizarre, and when I climbed Mt. Everest, it was perhaps stranger still, higher in fat and protein than at any other time in my life. In the death zone (above twenty-six thousand feet), I ate approximately 35 percent fat, 35 percent protein, and 30 percent carbohydrates, because my sole concern was to preserve as much muscle as I could, a futile but necessary effort at that altitude.

Occasionally, I have been in the middle of an endurance event and

found myself with no food whatsoever, but I've never suffered from it
—which isn't a surprise, as the human body can go for about three
weeks without food if it must. For adventure races, our team proac-
tively gained a pound of weight (fat) for every day we planned to be out
in the field, as we expected to lose a pound of body weight every day
during the race. Since we covered the equivalent of about fifty miles
per day, there was no way we could carry enough food to sustain us, so
we carried a pound of lighter-weight, high-calorie foods (e.g., cashews)
for us to eat each day. Yet during one eight-day Eco Challenge race, we
did run out of food on the first day, and we wound up splitting a cache
of M&Ms (three each—it was a party!) that sustained us over the next
two days until we reached our resupply cache. We were fine. Interest-
ingly, hunger persists for a little while and then the mind shuts the urge
off so you can go about your business. Then, when you regain access to
food, you become ravenous to make up for the deficit. Ah, instincts.

So I counsel you to engage in your own experiment of one. Pay
attention to what's working and what isn't, listen to your instincts and
your conscience, and be aware. Realize that your particular circumstances, environment, and genetics all matter. Case in point: more than
130 factors affect your blood-sugar response to different foods.[7] For
example, if you eat a banana and I eat a banana, each of our bodies
reacts in its own way, as if the fruit itself was different. Considering
that even this one biological response can vary so greatly, you have to
wonder how many other variables are at play and how highly individual
each of us is in how we digest, absorb, and metabolize the food we
consume. The best diet advice? Recognize and eschew the gimmicks,
know that all foods are okay in moderation, and then eat what is right
for *you*.

PART II

AIR

HEAD IN THE CLOUDS

Thousands of tired, nerve-shaken, over-civilized people are beginning to find out that going to the mountains is going home; that wilderness is a necessity; and that mountain parks and reservations are useful not only as fountains of timber and irrigating rivers, but as fountains of life.
—John Muir, naturalist

3

DARING

EMBARKING on an adventure like the one described below may seem ill-advised, but risk is surely in the gut of the beholder. There may be something you do in your life that would scare me silly, like singing in public, or teaching grad students, or performing heart surgery. Why do you do it? Probably for the same reason I take physical risks: because a life of complacency, bereft of challenge, is undeniably dull, and putting ourselves out there for something we love is where we find the juice. That's where we "live deep and suck the marrow out of life": in the pursuits that not only fire us up but also test our limits.

Risk is the price of exploration.
—Conrad Anker

RED. Red. Follow red. As if tailing hazard lights through the fog, I trained my eyes on the flashes of Rebecca Rusch's crimson cap bouncing into and out of view. Whenever she staggered, the bobber disappeared suddenly, sending me into a near-panic. She was having more trouble breathing than I was, but my vision had telescoped down to such a small field that I clung to every sight of her, hoping it would keep me moving forward and prevent me from blindly stumbling over the thousand-foot drop off the side of the mountain.

We were suffering from severe oxygen deprivation, having ascended to seventeen thousand feet in elevation over a period of hours. Still, Rebecca was moving, and I told myself that as long as I could follow her, I could keep on going.

This, my first experience with extreme altitude, resulted in a life-threatening condition. Both of us knew what was happening, as the signs are clear: first comes the weight on your chest, pressing so that you can't get enough air to power your brain or your body adequately, so all you can think about is how tired you are and how much you'd like to sit down on that rock over there. And then there's the headache, like someone has lassoed your skull and is slowly tightening the rope. Medically, here's what happens: cerebral edema, or swelling in the brain, blurs your eyesight, disorients and nauseates you, and tampers with your sanity. In the worst cases, it triggers seizures and can lead to death. Meanwhile, pulmonary edema, or fluid in the lungs, makes you feel as if you're drowning. You are, in fact, suffocating in thin air as the bloodstream remains deprived of oxygen while the breath can't sufficiently disperse carbon dioxide.

We were in Tibet, trying to get through one of many disciplines required during a Trans-Himalaya race, the Raid Gauloises in the spring of 2000, which was held on a course more than five hundred miles long and expected to take ten to twelve days to complete. The granddaddy of expedition races, a Raid Gauloises always included water crossings, long stretches on foot, some kind of climbing, and a riding sport—usually with a twist. In this case, we'd be mountain biking, riding an inflatable boogie board down rapids ("hydrospeed-ing"), whitewater river rafting, canoeing, canyoneering, and trekking. An annual "roving race" (which means they held it in a different locale each year), the Raid Gauloises was described by its organizers as "a sports-adventure-nature concept" that required "absolute self-suffi-ciency, total immersion in a natural environment in search of others, of oneself, and of another kind of life far from the usual everyday existence in our highly mechanized societies." To get a picture of what this was really like, it may help you to know it was the precursor to Mark Burnett's popular Eco-Challenge and, later, the relatively cushy reality show "Survivor."

My four teammates and I had begun this race near Xêgar (or *Shelkar Dzong*, Tibetan for "white crystal") at fourteen thousand feet and then ascended three thousand feet higher too quickly. I say *too quickly* because we weren't acclimated before we began. I'd spent the couple of days before we started just walking around the camp near Xêgar, sucking wind and needing to rest frequently. I'd also gotten rattled by realizing that if I didn't acclimate, my entire team could easily leave me in the dust. All were world-class athletes: Rebecca was a rock climber, Michael Kloser and Isaac Wilson were mountain bikers, and Patrick Harper was a cross-country skier; all were formidable paddlers, too. And then there was me: at nearly fifty, I was ten years older than Mike, and at least twenty years older than the rest. Heck, Isaac called me "Dad." An average cyclist and afraid of the water, at least I was a seasoned runner with a special talent for enduring extreme discomfort. Good thing, too, because we were in for it.

AFTER THE OFFICIAL start of the race, we took off on foot, heading through the village at top speed, the pointed peaks of the Himalayas on our right and in front of us, and Mount Everest in the far distance. Local children sent us off, waving orange flags and running with us for the first mile or so. We continued southwest, hustling up a gradual ascent that grew steeper and steeper. Soon, we reached an ancient monastery's stone wall, and then continued up and through the sacred place. The Tashilunpo monks, bald and wearing yellow robes, came out to greet us and wished us well, bowing their heads and smiling over their praying hands. *Namaste*. Up, up, up.

This doesn't feel so bad, I reassured myself. *Just breathe*. But as we progressed then transitioned to our mountain bikes, the exhilaration of starting a long, arduous journey wore off. After an agonizingly long stretch (something over fifty miles) we reached the next transition area and ditched the bikes, and then we moved forward on foot accompanied by a sturdy gray pony the race had assigned to our team.

None of us had prepared for the altitude especially. Nor did we pace ourselves, but it never occurred to us that extra measures would be necessary. Three of us had Vo_2 max tests showing over 80 ml/kg/min; a male in excellent health will be about two-thirds that rate, which means we were supremely fit and could utilize oxygen extraordinarily well. Still, Rebecca, Isaac, and I had been struggling with the altitude from the start, and things had gotten progressively worse as we approached seventeen thousand feet. The three of us took turns riding the pony as we gasped for air. Mike and Patrick seemed to hold their own and alternated leading the extremely good-natured animal, though all of us were breathing dust blown into our faces by the relentless wind. It stung our skin and raked our overtaxed lungs.

At the top of Yarle Shungla Pass, we made it to a yak herder's dung hut where we ducked inside for warmth. An hour later, we were in a quandary: go back out into the frozen night, backlit by a spectacular display of stars glistening far above a new dusting of snow, or stay inside where the foul-smelling smoke from the yak-crap fire was searing our eyes and lungs. We opted to get out in the fresh, frigid air and try to weave our way up to the next checkpoint, where we hoped to get medical attention and other aid. Once we stumbled into their sight, the race medics, who had been forewarned about our altitude sickness, rushed to check us with a pulse oximeter, and they quickly determined that we were hypoxic and should stop.

Drop out of the race, they counseled.

Rebecca, Isaac, and I were dangerously low on oxygen, and one of the medics pointed at me and pronounced, "He's out of his mind." Isaac waggled his thumb in my direction and murmured out of the side of his mouth, "He's *always* out of his mind," which broke the ice with the doc, who couldn't resist laughing at the joke. The medic reminded us that a normal pulse ox reading is ninety-five to a hundred, then announced that Rebecca's was in the fifties, and Isaac's and mine were in the sixties. We begged and pleaded with the medics, though, refusing and not wanting to quit. My thoughts wandered. What about the yaks we'd seen earlier in the day, subsisting on...what? Rocks? There was no grass, no vegetation at all to graze on, yet there they were, nibbling at the ground, when it looked as if there was nothing at all to sustain them. Our pony had seemed perfectly acclimated and content to haul our suffering bodies up the trail. What about the people, too, living at that altitude, adapted to their seemingly barren surroundings? If they could do it, couldn't we?

We were committed to continuing. We asked for a thirty-minute rest period, which the medics granted, and then they came back to give us an exam, a kind of high-altitude sobriety test, which Rebecca failed. Once again, they wanted to kick us out of the race. Despite our nearly breathless lungs and throbbing skulls, we argued and asked only for more rest. They relented, letting us use an old shuttle bus for at least an hour, after which they came and tried to kick us out of the race again.

Mike reasoned with the medics, making a persuasive case for letting us continue: soon, we'd be going down in altitude, which is the only real "treatment" for this sickness, anyway. (His ability to do this—to think straight and be a no-nonsense advocate in the middle of a crazy situation—was a key reason the rest of us wanted him on our team.) We all argued with the medics and refused to yield to the race doctors' wishes. Eventually, reluctantly, they gave us the go-ahead, knowing that Mike was right and we were on our way to lower ground and more plentiful oxygen.

One doc dogged us from a distance, watching our every move for a half mile. Just before he left us, he challenged, "Don't you really want to quit?"

Rebecca replied emphatically, *"No, I don't."*

After that, he left us alone. We continued to the crest of the hill, dragged ourselves over the top, and then started descending—just when we thought we were really done, things got easier. The lower we got, the better we felt. So long, altitude! We inhaled deeply, intensely relieved to feel the air fill our lungs. Now the toughest stage of the race was behind us. We continued trekking during various parts of the course. Over the next seven days, we did more mountain-biking, too, on dusty and rutted dirt roads, quickly descending thousands of feet. We trudged through snow, sleet, and freezing gusts. We swam through whitewaters and canoed on rapids, constantly being pulled under. We rappelled down waterfalls. Then we ran to the finish at the holy temple of Ram Janaki in Janakpur, Nepal.

(l to r) Mike Kloser, Isaac Wilson, me, Rebecca Rusch, and Patrick Harper.

It was a phenomenal race: Patrick had proven to be an extraordinary navigator, athlete, and voice of sanity and maturity throughout the expedition. Mike and Isaac had shone out, their solid paddling and mountain biking skills invaluable. Mike had even towed me on the mountain bike in the early stages, tying a bungee cord between his seatpost and my steering fork to help with a particularly tough incline. Rebecca recovered quickly below fifteen thousand feet and turned in stellar performances paddling, mountain biking, and rock climbing.

When my seventeen-year-old son, Taylor, saw me in Janakpur, he was frightened by the way I looked, and pulled away when I moved to hug him. "Dad, it looks like someone beat the crap out of you." He regarded me skeptically, searching my eyes as if he was trying to see if I was really myself. But in my elation and delusion, I thought I was in decent shape. Relief flooded over me—and with it gratitude. A truck had almost squeezed me off the road but had succeeded only in ripping through my sleeve to gash my arm. The rapids and rocks hadn't managed to drown me. I'd already coughed up most of the green gunk in my lungs. At some times during the race, I'd felt like the weakest link, but by the end, I'd whipped myself into fighting shape and torn through an epic mountain-bike ride in the second-to-last stage.

Reflecting on it all, though, I felt a long-held dream slipping away. Or, more accurately, I was putting it away. The difficulties I'd just endured made me swear off ever making an attempt on Mount Everest, which I'd wanted to climb for as long as I could remember. Since my childhood, I'd admired those pioneers who were the first to ascend to the highest peak in the world. In the 1950s and 1960s, my family and I had watched news coverage of these amazing expeditions, which at that time occurred only about once every two years. Grizzled climbers came down chastened and in some cases maimed by *Chomolungma*, the dead remained frozen on the mountainside, and it seemed an adventure even to contemplate scaling it. As a child, I'd promised myself: *Someday.* Yet here I was, standing in the shadow of that giant, wrecked by the altitude of its established base at only seventeen thousand feet. How could I hope to ascend into the death zone above twenty-six thousand feet, much less all the way to the top at 29,035 feet? To put it plainly, I was now scared of the altitude and thought there was little chance I'd ever overcome its stifling, suffocating, blinding pressures.

So I consoled myself: We'd handled each of the new challenges as they'd come, on the water and over land, taking rest where we could and leaning on each other when necessary, course-correcting once or twice, and pushing ourselves to move up from a double-digit ranking into the top ten out of more than sixty teams. Ultimately, we finished the Trans-Himalaya race as the highest ranking all-American team ever in the Raid Gauloises.

Everest, though? Forget it.

W HEN YOU'RE ASCENDING any mountain, literal or figurative, the core principle is acclimation. It means incremental progress, occasionally having to back down when the air gets too thin and chokes you with fear, and then climbing even higher when you've adjusted. A friend of mine who's known mostly for his extraordinary spec homes—meaning he creates multimillion-dollar mansions without a buyer in mind, which is a daredevil financial move—has said this about risks: to take the big ones, you have to start small. Frank McKinney insists, "You must exercise your risk tolerance like a muscle." It's another way of getting at this idea of acclimation.

He started out in the 1980s with a $50,000 fixer-upper, then over more than twenty years, gradually moved up to the stratospheric price point he operates in today. Likewise, I didn't go from zero to the Raid Gauloises. Starting in 1979, I challenged myself as a runner by entering my first 10K race, then eventually moved up to half-marathons, then marathons, then fifty-milers, then twenty-four-hour races, then hundred-milers, and went farther still after that. By the time I arrived at that Raid Gauloises in 2000, I'd set records for extreme distances in extreme conditions, and completed several other adventure races with respectable finish times.

So here's my point: it is absolutely worthwhile to take a risk, but the smart risk isn't some flight of fancy. It's crucial before you embark on something to be grounded in the realities of your own ability to handle it. You need to strike a balance between the uncertainty of "Can I do this thing?" and the likelihood that you can, between the potential challenges and rewards.

Adventure teaches you to recognize your limits even while you're pushing the boundaries. This is especially true with any adventure that involves physical risk-taking. And this is the kind I can tell you about with some authority: deciding to be bold in some way, taking physical risks of any kind even if they're only slightly out of the box, expands not only your sense of self but also your worldview.

I haven't always championed this idea. Despite their formidable strength, Clara and Elmer Ulrich—my stalwart, entrepreneurial parents—were surprisingly risk-averse, extremely cautious about anything unfamiliar, and I went along up to a point. My mother and father didn't like to see us kids do anything they considered dangerous, so when I announced one day that I wanted to attend flight school and become a pilot, they both balked and tried to talk me out of it. At the time, I was a two-stripe airman first class in the National Guard, learning to fix aircraft guidance equipment at an Air Force technical/aviation school in Biloxi, Mississippi. Mom and Dad's protests grew louder after I took a few flying classes, and I acquiesced to their fears and quit. Even today, I'm still kicking myself for not having learned to fly, but I did get a significant lesson from this experience: a few years after that happened, I determined that I would never again let someone else's fears—or, to a great extent, the fearful voice in my own head—make my decisions for me. Instead, it became central to my identity to explore new places and test myself, to find out what I was made of and, more important, discover *who I am* when I'm tested.

Consider this description from *Psychology Today* of the rewards of taking physical risks.

Beyond developing self-confidence, physical risk-taking can actually stretch your very identity. As Carthage College sociology professor Stephen Lyng explains it, risk-taking jumpstarts people who feel pushed along through life in limited, prescribed roles. Self-determination in the face of uncertainty helps develop a strong sense of self. "It comes from having to improvise a response to the challenge at hand," says Lyng. **"Once you are in the realm of uncertainty, anything is possible in terms of how you think about yourself."** When we're confronted with this kind of "experiential anarchy," he explains, we're able to see how the patterns in our everyday lives may be holding us back.

The best way to reap the benefits of physical risk-taking is to make it a habit. "The more practice you have in situations where you have to make rapid decisions with great consequence, the more likely you are to be able to act rather than freeze," says Cline. This is the idea behind all sorts of training, from CPR to fire drills to combat maneuvers.[1] [Emphasis added.]

The article goes on to identify three types of people—risk avoiders, risk reducers, and risk optimizers—and to prescribe actions for each:

- If you generally *avoid risk,* then **unsettle your status quo.**
  Do something different than you normally would do. For
  example, if you usually run on paved roads, give the trail a
  try, and if you usually vacation in hotels, go camping with
  your family. Walk the kids to school instead of driving. Let
  curiosity expose you to something *new.*
- If you generally *reduce risk,* then **do something that scares
  you a little.** Push yourself. Find an endeavor that makes
  you feel both nervous and excited, and then get some
  coaching on how to pursue it. Talk with someone who has
  achieved the thing you'll attempt, get advice, and put
  together a plan. Follow the plan and surprise yourself by
  doing something you never thought you could.
- If you tend to *optimize risk,* then **keep on going.** Find new
  ways to challenge yourself. Switch sports. Try some solo
  endeavors. Do something other people will think is crazy.
  Build a lifestyle and a life of adventure.

One of the greatest gifts my wife Heather has given me has been to
accept me fully, to acknowledge without condemnation that I'm one of
the "risk optimizers." I'm not right for being this way, nor am I wrong
for being this way. You're neither right nor wrong for whatever level of
risk you're willing to accept or seek in your own life, and I'm not at all
trying to convince you to change who you are.

At the same time, I'm encouraging you to reject whatever limitations you or someone else has artificially imposed upon you. Even if
you fail or fall, even if you temporarily reject your dreams instead of
your limitations, as I did. (Surprise! I eventually summited Mount
Everest, but I detail that story later.) Realize, accept, and then celebrate that we humans can acclimate to nearly any environment: high or
low elevation, scorching or frigid temperatures, arid or humid, rocky or
grassy or desert sand. *Do* get out and experience them all to whatever
degree you can. *Do* prepare and understand what you're getting into,
but *don't* overthink it. *Don't* talk yourself out of something incredible.
Be willing to put yourself in an uncomfortable position on purpose,
then follow through by acting as if you've always planned to succeed.

You'll either be surprised at how well you manage it or discover that it's too much—or both, which is perhaps the best possible outcome. You'll not only survive the elements, but you'll find yourself strengthened, have a heightened awareness of your surroundings, and be more connected with both nature and humanity. I promise.

4

ACCLIMATION

TWO PERFECTLY GOOD reasons I never should have become a mountaineer: 1) altitude sickness is horrible, and 2) I'm afraid of heights—the chest-pounding, flop-sweating, immobilizing kind of afraid. This means any overlook at a high elevation could simultaneously wreck me psychologically and weaken me physically, leaving me shaking with fear, feeling as if I'm wracked with the flu while trying to breathe through a straw. Climb in that condition? Heck, it's hard just to imagine surviving the next inhale.

After my particularly nasty bout of acute mountain sickness in the Himalayas, I'd sworn off extreme altitude. But less than a year later, I started pining for Mount Everest again. I'd longed to make this climb since I was a little boy, and the lure of the summit was stronger than my memories of nausea, headaches, and total disorientation. I told a few people, including at least one journalist, that this was my idea of the ultimate adventure, that reaching the top would be a dream fulfilled. In the short article he wrote about me, mostly to do with running records and adventure racing, he included my desire to scale Everest, tossed into the last paragraph like an afterthought, which I think he meant to make my other athletic efforts seem more impressive. Playing up my credentials as "The Endurance King," he called this aspiration *humdrum* by comparison.

True, more people have seen the top of Everest than will complete some of the torturous things I've done, but it is hardly a casual commitment. The recent fad of "everyone" climbing the Great Mountain (the only impediments seeming to be the money and time to do it) had gotten plenty of people thinking it was no big deal, including some who lead amateur expeditions. This showed a critical misunderstanding of the mountain, climbing, and the perils of high altitude.

No matter what anyone else had to say about it, I was plenty scared of the whole enterprise, so I just kept pining. It would remain a dream deferred, I thought. Soon after that article ran in *Outside* magazine's December 2001 issue, though, I received a letter from a mountaineer who lived nearby. He'd read the piece, thought we had a lot in common and should meet, and offered to help me in my quest. He included his phone number and said I could call any time. Intrigued, I wondered if this guy was the real deal.

Turns out he was. In 1986, Gary Scott had set the world record for the fastest ascent of the tallest mountain in North America, Denali in Alaska (formerly known as Mount McKinley). In just 18.5 hours, he'd gone from seven thousand feet at base camp to the top of the 20,237-foot mountain at an unprecedented pace, and he'd done it *by himself:* solo and unsupported, without supplemental oxygen. Gary has since written about Denali (the mountain has officially gone back to its Native Alaskan name, which means "the high one"), outlining its characteristics and dangers:

> ...no other mountain on earth towers as high over its base as Denali (plus, due to the reduced depth of the atmosphere at the poles, it feels more like 23,000 feet would feel in the Himalayas). I have a good friend who lost all his fingers and toes to frostbite on Denali, and another who took fifty-six days to climb it due to horrendously bad weather. Climbing Denali involves surviving huge crevasses, ferocious storms, and extremely cold conditions.[1]

He did more than survive. His was the first ascent completed in one day, and his record went unchallenged for nearly three decades.[2] As he neared the highest elevations, he moved so efficiently that his "feet barely cleared the surface of the snow" and he completely relaxed so that he didn't use "an extra molecule of oxygen"—his body became "a huge moving lung."[3] What's more, he did the whole thing on two Mars bars, two bagels, and two quarts of water—and without the advantage of the lightweight equipment we have today.[4]

Of course, I didn't know any of this when I called him the first time. I didn't know much about Denali, either, except that in my mind it dwarfed all other mountains but Everest. Having read *Call of the Wild* over and over again as a boy, I imagined Denali towering over Alaska— land of gold, glory, and long dark nights, where sled dogs' paws pound the ice, and their crystallized breath billows through the carved-out wilderness. So, yes, I had some romantic notions. Yet I also had practical reasons for being frightened and writing off my aspirations as merely fantasies.

In our conversation, Gary acknowledged what a big deal it is to consider tackling any great mountain. He'd climbed Everest, he told me, and he certainly did not dismiss it as humdrum. In his first attempt to reach the top, he'd spent the night below the summit and barely survived. The second attempt to go all the way up was also thwarted, with him trying to rescue a Sherpa, only to have the man die in the icefall, and Gary being plagued thereafter with severe mental and physical anguish. Knowing better than most how daunting Everest could be, he advised me to get some relevant experience before entertaining the idea of tackling Everest. He suggested a good first step would be to put together a team and go up Denali together; he'd be our guide, and I could invite a couple of people to come with us.

His friendly voice with its cheery Australian accent, along with his obvious competence, built my confidence. Even after I confessed my reservations about going above eighteen thousand feet (the point at which I'd become seriously ill before), he assured me that I'd learn a great deal on Denali, including the final summit push from 17,000 to 20,237 feet. Because I was already physically fit enough but needed to work on my skills and approach, he'd help me get some more mountaineering experience before heading to Alaska, and then we'd go after it. Most significant, we'd handle the altitude by properly acclimating, something I had completely neglected during the trans-Himalayan race. We'd spend a day at base camp, then work our way up the mountain over the course of about three weeks.

Do this, I inferred, *and Everest might be within my reach.*

Well, Denali would be a test, anyway. Even with Gary's pep talk, I was still scared shitless. I was also—perhaps for the first time in my fifty years—concerned about how my decision would affect someone else. Previously, I'd run roughshod over other people's feelings, either neglecting to include them in my decision-making or shutting them out altogether. My sweetheart and soon-to-be wife, Heather Vose, had just moved in with me, and Gary understood when I told him I didn't want to put her through weeks of uncertainty and fear for my life. He reassured me that we wouldn't do anything foolish, that we'd be as safe as possible.

"Okay," I said. "I'll think about it and get back to you."

In the wake of Gary's enthusiasm, I hung up the phone in disbelief. *Is this really happening? Can Gary help me? Will I get over my own fears and go for it?* Heather and I discussed it over several days (during which Gary called to reassure her), and eventually she green-lighted the idea. Not only that, but she agreed to fly out and meet me in Alaska when it was over. This was an amazing gesture on her part, given her own history with the place: during the winter of 1990, she'd spent seventeen hours in the Bering Sea after her boat capsized in a storm, and she hadn't been back to Alaska since.

That accident was probably the most painful experience of Heather's life. Having left port with three other people, she'd watched two of her colleagues fall victim to hypothermia then drown during the night. She didn't know it at the time, but the captain had made it to shore, so she spent hours alone in the frigid water until morning finally arrived. She survived by forcing herself to eat what was available— some soggy Triscuits and a bit of juice from a can of beef stew— holding back her tears for fear of dehydration. At last, about seventeen hours after the boat had flipped, a rescue team extracted her from the overturned Boston Whaler, traumatized but alive.

My wife, Heather, the day of her horrific boating accident near Adak island in 1990.

Reflecting on what she'd been through made my fear of altitude sickness seem insignificant, but each of us knew we'd have to move beyond the past if this new endeavor were to succeed. We both thought we could do it. We were willing to try.

The idea took hold of me the way things like this sometimes do, consuming most of my conscious thoughts and setting up camp in my subconscious, too. I daydreamed about Denali during waking hours; I dreamed about it at night while I was sleeping. I dreamed about it all the time. My mind churned: *Can I do this? Is it too dangerous? Am I fit enough? Will the altitude crush me again?* And in the next moment: *Yes, I can do this! I can pull this off. I'm definitely ready for it. The mountain gods will smile upon me, and I won't get sick. With the help of a little luck, I make my own success.*

I visualized myself on the mountain, climbing with friends, feeling strong, capable, healthy. I began to convince myself that what I imagined could be real, and I wanted it more than ever. Although I knew the possibility for failure existed, it started not to matter much in the face of all the exhilarating possibilities.

Denali demanded that I confront my fears and my unpleasant past, move beyond them, and then approach this adventure fresh and full of possibility instead of anxiety and doubt. I coached myself: Tame the mind and train the body. Make the difficult choice, and just go for it. Take this step, and then consider the next. *Acclimation* was the new watchword: on the mountain, I would let my body do what it was built to do, to *adjust*, to learn to breathe that thin air, to be stable and strong in a new environment. Hello again, altitude. My mind would have to adjust, too, learn to accept new heights and then keep on going.

So I said yes to Denali.

We invited a few others to join us: Tony Di Zinno, my friend and a professional photographer who was known for his shots of the Eco Challenge adventure races; and Charlie Engle,[5] a fellow I'd met during some of the adventure racing I'd done. Gary invited his new pal Aron Ralston to assist him in guiding us. The two of them had met when Aron attended one of Gary's lectures, and they'd hit it off. Gary thought Aron's experience climbing in the Rockies would make him a good right-hand man for Denali. It probably didn't hurt that they were both as fun-loving as they were serious about climbing, that they both oozed confidence and were straight shooters.

When Gary first introduced us, Aron was twenty-six, still pretty green but clearly had strong innate abilities and had studied the mountains. One morning, Aron and I went out to Pikes Peak, and that's when I first realized how strong he was. Going from sixty-three hundred feet to over fourteen thousand, the ascent is half a marathon's length, 13.32 miles at an average of 11 percent grade. Although he told me he wasn't much of a runner, Aron kept pace with me up and down over five or six hours on a course I'd run dozens of times. I'd set the record for a Pikes Peak Quad, meaning I ran up and down the mountain four times for the equivalent of four marathon distances. This was my turf, and he had no trouble keeping up. *Holy shit,* I thought. *Who is this guy?*

ARON'S BOOK *Between a Rock and a Hard Place,* which he wrote after a
horrific experience in 2003—a year *after* we went to Alaska together—
tells the story of the hardship he endured while trapped in an isolated
slot canyon. It reveals a horrifying truth: he could escape death only by
doing the unthinkable, severing his arm. Could you do it? Would you
do it? Cut off your arm to save your life? It's likely you would. Because
at our most vulnerable, and our most heroic, we all have the grit. It
may take a while to summon the courage. We may fight the idea of
doing what we know we must, but in the end, most people will take on
even the hardest thing when it means survival. A wolverine will chew
off its own foot to escape a trap; most animals, including humans, have
these life-saving, essential instincts. Some will fight harder than others,
and a few will give up, but all of us have the capability to save
ourselves.

Sometimes, making solid decisions when faced with difficult
circumstances is not about literal survival, but instead about the
survival of your best self, the self aligned with what you believe is most
important, most valuable, most meaningful. This is why, for example,
decisions about marriage and divorce can be so agonizing, or the question of whether to have children or not can be so fraught, or choosing
the "best" place to live can be so difficult. That's at least part of what
Aron's tale is about: having the *cojones* to do what you must, especially
when it's incredibly hard. If you've seen the film *127 Hours,* which is
based on Aron's book, you know this movie isn't for everyone, because
it's graphic and because you have to sit for an hour and a half in
extremis watching Aron, played dead-on by James Franco, and feel the
emotional tension of *will he? won't he? how could he?* even though we all
know he eventually did. But to reduce this story to something at the
end of Aron's arm, or rather something no longer at the end of Aron's
arm, is to miss the point.

What's so amazing to me isn't that Aron did this horrific thing,
but that he kept his wits about him during what happened next. I
am most impressed that he was able to get out of the canyon,
wounded but with an improvised tourniquet, keep himself hydrated
(by drinking his own urine), and eventually find help. *He survived.*
Ultimately, the amputation was a pragmatic decision about

preserving himself, the only thing to do. And yes, you'd do it, too. Others have.

One winter, a man hiking near my house at St. Mary's Glacier got caught under a boulder, cut off his lower leg, crawled for a mile on the trail, and then drove his Jeep down the road so he wouldn't perish in an oncoming storm. What finally gave Aron the push to do the thing he dreaded was a compelling vision, a "premonition" of himself with a child, the future. It urged him to save himself, shouted the essential message in his ear: YOU CAN'T FAIL YOURSELF. *Do the hard thing.*

A while back, I watched a video of philosopher Ruth Chang talking about "How to Make Hard Choices." In it, she revealed why making pro and con lists—something Aron certainly did while contemplating his next move—can be so unhelpful. They don't always reveal the better choice because sometimes there isn't one, such as when you're deciding who (or whether) to marry, or what profession to pursue after college, or if you want to try something new. The most powerful question you can ask yourself when making a tough choice is *What do I stand for?* Chang asserts that this is the *only meaningful question* to ask yourself.

People who don't exercise their normative powers in hard choices are drifters.... Drifters allow the world to write the story of their lives. They let mechanisms of reward and punishment—pats on the head, fear, the easiness of an option—determine what they do. So the lesson of hard choices: reflect on what you can put your agency behind, what you can be *for.* Through hard choices, become that person. **Far from being sources of agony and dread, hard choices provide an opportunity to celebrate what is special about the human condition,** that the reasons that govern our choices as correct or incorrect sometimes run out, and it is here, in the space of hard choices, that we have the power to create reasons for ourselves to become the distinctive people that we are.[6] [Emphasis added.]

People have asked me repeatedly why I pursue such "crazy" athletic accomplishments, why I become compelled by pursuits that are so risky or difficult. The only real answer I have ever been able to produce is that it is just who I am. I love the experience of pushing myself, even if it is temporarily painful, especially if it expands my sense of self and

my abilities, and (forgive me if this is grandiose) expands my percep-
tions of the capabilities of the human race. When you bring this down
to the essential principle, I'm not so different from anyone else. For
every one of us, *experiences and not acquisitions are what last;* material
things are expendable, and what we accomplish in life is everlasting; no
one can ever take that away.

Psychologists continue to study why experiences are so much more
gratifying than material things, but the question of which yields more
"enduring happiness" has been settled: it's experiences. One of the
reasons this is true is that you enjoy the anticipation of the experience,
the experience itself (usually), and the nostalgia for the experience
afterward (you can even re-imagine an unpleasant experience and turn
it into a sweet memory), while *things* tend to make us impatient to get
them, bring us some delight when we acquire them, and then are
forgotten or taken for granted once they're in our possession. The
other reason is that experiences don't invite comparison with other
people in the way that stuff does. In one study, it was noted that many
people can't decide if they would rather earn a big salary but less than
their peers, or earn a modest salary but more than their peers. With an
experience, there's no waffling. "Would you rather have two weeks of
vacation when your peers get only one? Or four weeks when your peers
get eight? People choose four weeks with little hesitation," the scientists say.[7]

Knowing what you stand for, then putting the full weight of that
understanding behind the preparation and realization of an experience
that expresses it, can be one of the most rewarding things you will ever
do. Acting on *inspiration* makes you feel fully alive—the word itself
means both to draw a breath and to heed the call of creativity.
Knowing that, I urge you to consider what puts the fire in your belly.
What fascinates you? What can't you get out of your mind?

IN PREPARATION for our trip to Alaska, Tony Di Zinno ramped up his
personal training to include some long hikes with a backpack, and he
had a crash course on crevasse rescue and traveling while roped up and

using crampons on ice and snow. He was living in California and travelling a lot on photography assignments, and he did what he could to
push himself. Tony was in excellent shape, but he compared himself to
the rest of us by saying he was like a six-banger Studebaker trying to
keep up with a bunch of V-8 Porsches. Charlie and I were both
familiar with ropes and crampons from adventure racing, and we were
indeed at a fitness level to take on pretty much anything. I upped my
running mileage to eighty miles per week, continued multiday adventure racing—great for conditioning and getting further experience
with carrying gear over long distances—and had some excursions with
Gary and Aron to work on conditioning and altitude coping skills.

During one trip, we went to St. Mary's Glacier and yoked ourselves
together with about forty feet of rope between us. We did some
crampon work, and I learned to keep my feet disentangled from one
another, deliberately picking them up as I moved up and down the
mountain, sidestepping and carefully crossing one foot over the other,
then setting the crampon teeth flat on the slope, kicking steps in to
stabilize myself and leave a clear footprint for those behind, and
ascending especially steep slopes by driving just the front two teeth
into the ice. We also practiced ice-ax arrests: The slider would shout,
"Falling!" and the rest of us would thrust ourselves forward, digging our
axes deep into the snow in an effort to tighten the rope and stop the
fall. We were teaching ourselves to react quickly, to preserve ourselves
without hesitation.

Gary shared with us some of the black humor of Denali to help us
understand how important this gear and safety training was to a trip up
the mountain: On the West Buttress between fourteen thousand and
seventeen thousand feet, one of the steep side hills has been named
the "Orient Express" because Asian climbers, wearing booties instead
of their climbing boots, reportedly had stepped out of their tents
there, and away they went to their deaths. Similarly, the "Autobahn"
just above seventeen thousand feet is supposedly the site where some
Europeans attempted to summit using ski poles instead of ice axes,
started to slide, and then couldn't self-arrest.

Our group outings were important because I got to know Gary
better and grew to trust and admire him not only as an athlete but also

as a mountaineer who deeply respected the history of his sport. He
sometimes shared his ideas about "clean" or "pure" climbing, doing it
the way the old-timers had without a lot of extra gear or supplemental
oxygen. No doubt he knew how anxious we were, so he also joked with
us, peering through his round glasses and furrowing his brow when he
was trying to make a point.

Our team was taking shape: Aron, this astonishingly able climber;
Tony, the cautious but curious voice of reason; Charlie, who was
spring-loaded for anything; and Gary, who made me think almost
nothing could get in the way of us standing on the very top of the
frozen North.

In June of 2002, we gathered in Talkeetna, Alaska at the Fairview
Inn, a local watering hole and boarding house in this historic village
where almost all climbers start their expeditions up Denali. All of us
were ready to go, fit and game. Everyone but Gary was also a bit naive,
scared, and looking for someone to keep us safe on that huge mountain. Each of us had our own reasons for climbing: for the challenge, to
explore uncertainty or overcome our inadequacies, to document and
show the mountain and climbers' personalities with pictures, to prove
ourselves, and/or for the adventure. Tony said that he wanted to put
his money where his mouth was; he called himself an adventure
photographer, but had yet to prove to himself that he was. He looked
at Denali as a chance to make that claim real.

Later, as we lounged around our equipment and waited for the
planes to fly us up to base camp, I thought we didn't look much like
mountaineers; we seemed more like a random bunch of guys who'd tied
one on the night before. Always the professional, though, Gary got
right to work, organizing us even as he tried to loosen us up a bit. It
was clear that he didn't take himself or any of us too seriously. He
respected the mountain thoroughly, though, and he would be undeterred by any challenge or rocky path. Despite his boyish look, he was
clearly a leader. Just being around him set the rest of us immediately at
ease and made us eager to load up. Together we packed over 675
pounds of gear on two planes, enough for each of us to carry 135
pounds between a sled and backpack once we hit the ice. We divided
into two groups, with Aron and me getting the first flight over; the

plane would return for the others, and we'd all be together at the end of the day to set up camp near the landing strip on Kahiltina Glacier.

Flying over the Alaska Range, the bush pilot weaved our plane between the tall peaks, rarely going much higher than a couple of thousand feet above the valley. He casually pointed out a plane wreck at the bottom of the snow slope where we'd land, and when we cleared the downed craft by a matter of feet, he helpfully instructed, "That's what you don't want to do when you're landing a bird." Amused but anxious, I managed a half-hearted laugh.

Despite attempts to fully regain my calm once we were on the ground, I was getting even more worked up. Although I'd completed many athletic endeavors since that insanity in the Himalayas—adventure races, a 584-mile back and forth four times across Death Valley with two ascents of Mount Whitney—and hundreds of recreational ascents of Colorado's fourteeners (mountain peaks of at least fourteen thousand feet), I hadn't been above eighteen thousand feet. Not once had I attempted to tackle high altitude again.

So, as soon as we deplaned and unloaded the gear, I started shoveling snow and pitching tents and generally working my ass off, trying to make myself useful and burn nervous energy. (Denali's base camp is just a landing strip with the surrounding area covered by snow and ice: no restrooms, no running water, no tidy campsites, so there's plenty to be done to make it habitable.) By the time the rest of the team arrived, I was feeling shaky and knew I was starting to suffer from mountain sickness already. *But why?* We were at seven thousand feet in elevation, barely high enough to make even the most sensitive person ill. Some people start experiencing symptoms at eight thousand, but maybe I had become more susceptible somehow? Soon, I was throwing up and then feeling my skull tighten. *Oh, no,* I lamented to myself. *It's happening all over again. All the planning and preparation and expectation...it's over and I haven't even gotten started yet.* Imagine my relief when Gary assured me it was only sun poisoning. He told me to get into my tent and ride it out. "That's not smart to be doing so much so soon," he chided.

The irony was a bit much: having repeatedly run hundreds of miles in the hottest place on earth—Death Valley, where temps are regularly above 115 degrees and sometimes reach above 130—I travel to Alaska and get taken down by severe sun exposure within hours. It just goes to show you that sometimes, the best thing to do is take it slow, familiarize yourself with the environment, and then take the next steps when it's prudent. (Isn't this the principle of acclimation applied to something other than altitude?) What I didn't know until then is that, on the glacier, the UV rays bounce off the reflective surface of the snow, hitting anyone standing on it from above and below. There's simply no escaping it unless you shield yourself completely, and covering up never crossed my mind, as the weather was beautiful otherwise—warm enough to be in shirt sleeves but with the ice emitting a deceptive coolness all around.

Luckily, recovery didn't take too long. After spending the night with a pounding headache and nausea, I finally fell asleep around the same time the sun rose at 3:00 a.m., and I emerged from my tent around 10:00 a.m., depleted but functional at least. Everyone else was busy busting camp and packing up to leave, and by noon we were walking away from base camp, following tracks that headed up the glacier toward our next camp a couple of miles and two thousand feet higher. The route was obvious, as the glacier we followed was much like going up a frozen river in a valley.

That night, the sun went down in a blaze of orange, painting the white landscape with shades of coral, apricot, and copper. I finally started to relax.

From then on, each day we continued moving up the mountain. Whereas a few of the other big mountains have local people or pack animals who can help with the load (the porters on Kilimanjaro, the Sherpas on Everest, the mules on Aconcagua), we carried everything ourselves, hauling about 120 pounds of gear each, with fifty in a backpack and the rest on a sled. My sled was tricked out, too.

Sleds just like that were available for free on the glacier, used and discarded over and over again, but at this stage of my life, I wasn't willing to risk falling off the side of a mountain just to pinch a penny. So I browsed catalogs and websites for something more substantial, and when my wife Heather saw a picture of those pricey mountain sleds, she said they looked an awful lot like the relatively inexpensive ones she'd seen used for ice fishing while she was growing up in

Minnesota; all we'd need to do is add some skids to keep it from tipping over. So, after I bought myself a fishing sled from Cabela's, I screwed some aluminum doorjambs to the bottom (the perfect shape and weight to dig into the snow in the back but glide over the ice in the front), and I think mine turned out to be top-of-the-line, custom-fit, and solid as a rock.

Pulling my sled and carrying my gear on Denali in 2002.

We lugged freeze-dried food, sleeping bags, sleeping pads, ice axes, snow shoes, sunglasses, trekking poles, down jackets, helmets, crampons, stoves, fuel, tents, and shovels. A shovel might seem counter to the mountaineering mantra of *pack light,* but it's a crucial piece of equipment. If you're stuck in a storm, you use that shovel to build a wall to deflect some of the cold and wet, or dig a better toilet. Heck, you could stave off the boredom by making snow sculptures. In truth, much of mountaineering is biding your time. Plans and people move forward at the whim of the weather, so plenty of time gets spent just waiting for the right conditions.

Sure enough, we endured a couple of snow dumps while we were at the twelve-thousand-foot camp, the first lasting a couple of days, and the second coming soon thereafter and lasting through another night. We woke up and dug ourselves up out of two to four feet of snow.

When we reached seventeen thousand feet, we got socked in again. We'd been steadily moving up toward this last milestone for close to two weeks, anxiously anticipating our summit push, when the severe weather quite literally made us chill out. Howling winds battered our tents, and snow flattened them into something the size of a crawl space under a house, less than a couple of feet high. We had to wait for a change before attempting the final ascent. Our plan was to make the climb from seventeen thousand to the top and back down to seventeen thousand in a day, but that day would have to wait.

Meanwhile, Aron was in bad shape after leading Tony, Charlie, and me up above the high camp to do a gear drop. He was suffering from gastroenteritis: vomiting, diarrhea, and a fever. Dehydration and lack of appetite weakened him further, sending his health into serious decline, and he finally relented and went back down to fourteen thousand feet to recuperate. Once he felt better, he planned to try to come up again. It probably didn't help that he'd been hauling a heavy pack laden with Phish CDs and abundance of camera equipment, which he'd dropped on the West Buttress and planned to retrieve later. When Gary saw the load and insisted that Aron pare it way down, Aron never complied, secretly hauling two dozen CDs up the mountainside.

Within a day or so, Gary went down the mountain to get Aron's pack and discovered Aron's stash, which made him angry as hell. He had another shock during that trip, too, almost sliding into a fatal fall on the Orient Express when he accidentally hooked one of his crampon teeth onto his atrea, a daisy chain attached to the climbing harness. In an instant, he realized that the more he stepped down, the more likely he was to fall, so he counterintuitively raised his foot to free himself. He was visibly rattled when he returned to high camp, Aron's weighty pack in hand.

Around this time, I had an epiphany: I was okay. We'd made it. The three rookies and Gary hadn't gotten sick! Tony, Charlie, and I were feeling good and champing at the bit. But most important: we had acclimated! There, at seventeen thousand feet on Denali, I realized that what had happened in the past was fully behind me, and right then, in the present moment, I was ready to go even higher.

Indeed, the height of Denali wasn't frightening anymore, as I thought I could reach the summit without ill effects from the altitude. There was the threat of storms or extreme wind possibly blowing us off the mountain, as well as other dangers, but still. Now that I was in the environment, I discovered that I could handle myself, and the prospect of danger was no longer so paralyzing. It's strange how that plays out in so many situations: once an adventure is underway, the fear dissipates and the concentration takes over. It's another kind of acclimation, an adaptation to the environment, another example of the brain's amazing plasticity.

After Gary returned to camp with Aron's pack, he was ready to guide us up the mountain. We remained holed up in our tents for a day while the wind howled, but the next morning, the door opened for us to make our summit push, so we stepped through it. It took about five hours to go all the way up. Gary had made sure that we'd spent enough time at each camp so we were well acclimated, but I was still amazed at how I gasped for air at that altitude. We solidified as a team and worked together as we became more and more confident that we would make it to the top. Still, the question of making the summit or not lingered, as the weather could have changed rapidly or someone might have gotten sick and would have had to go down, which would have meant everyone would go down as our only experienced climber was Gary, and he'd have to accompany anyone who took ill. The truth is that summiting is always a crapshoot.

After a couple hours of climbing, we became more confident we had everything we needed to summit, so we dropped some gear on the high-altitude snow slope called the Football Field, which allowed us to travel faster. The weather cooperated (the mountain gods smiled upon us!) and we were all business. Our focus was on the next step, the next breath, not getting too far ahead of ourselves, but looking off in the distance trying to make out the top, where it was, if we could see it. Focus was narrow but expanded. As we approached the summit, a huge sense of accomplishment began to flood over us all, and, when we got to the top, it was like one big photoshoot and celebration. The 360-degree view was spectacular as we looked down on the glaciers below, which looked like huge ice rivers flowing down the valleys. We were patting ourselves on the back, figuratively and literally. We spoke of what a huge accomplishment it was and how grateful we were to have shared such a meaningful experience.

Of course, we were all elated after reaching the top. Remarkably, there's cell phone service up there, as it is within line of sight, and we were so high as to ping a tower. In tears, Tony called his grandfather, who had always been a great support system for him over the years and shared the great news. I remember hearing bits and pieces of the conversation: his grandfather said he couldn't be prouder of Tony and all his accomplishments. This was the icing on the cake.

My mother had a very different reaction when I called her. When I told her that I had made it to the top of Denali, she chastised me. "What are you doing up there? You'd better get down right away!" That was entirely in character for her, as she always thought these sorts of things were too dangerous and that I really ought to be at home tending to the family business.

To be honest, my spirits dropped after that, and I got pretty quiet and introspective, but I will say this: the peak of Denali ain't a bad place to take a moment for private reflection. At the top, you realize how high you are: above twenty thousand feet, you see these extraordinarily huge glaciers going on for miles. Off the side, there's the Great Gorge of Ruth Glacier, one of the deepest canyons in the world, filled with ice and twice the size of the Grand Canyon. Far off in the distance, you can see greenery, but it's twenty to thirty miles away. You are a speck on an enormous chunk of white ice, settled into the vast field of our world, nestled into but one corner of our inconceivably huge universe. I like that feeling—we humans are so small, so insignificant, but part of something mind-blowingly enormous. It is a paradoxical expansion and contraction, a contradictory sense of insignificance and greatness, of finiteness and boundlessness, of solitude and connectedness.

After reaching the summit, we headed down to the high camp and spent the night. The next day we made a beeline all the way down the mountain to low base camp. It was a long, long way down, but we were excited to return and get on the plane back to Talkeetna. We'd spent nearly three weeks above the treeline, the frozen landscape completely barren of greenery. When we finally dipped to three thousand feet and our eyes took in the first signs of plant life again, we were stunned. Staring at the verdant vegetation, I felt like a starved man tasting his first bites of food—ecstatic and insatiable. Who knew merely *looking* at leaves could feel like this? We boarded the plane and ascended to glide among the mountaintops to which we'd become so accustomed in such a short time, but as soon as we descended and disembarked, with the clouds suddenly above instead of below us, the musty smells from decaying ground cover, smoke from nearby houses, and aromas of cooking from restaurants filled the air. We reached down to touch the ground, the grass familiar but temporarily exotic and thrilling. It all felt so good to soak in the sights and sounds using all of our senses that we had been deprived of using.

Our thoughts turned to seeing the people we loved, to taking a shower, to getting a good burger. We were sick of crowding into our small cramped tents and marinating in the smell of each other. (Since then, I prefer climbing with women as they are much more civil and don't smell as raunchy as men do.) And then, only a day later, spotting Heather and taking her in my arms at the airport were the ultimate triumphal moments. I'd done it! And I'd come back to her. It was fun to surprise her there, as she had no idea I'd be able to meet her in Anchorage; in fact, Charlie helped me fool her a bit by meeting her at the gate, explaining that I'd sent him to check on her and make sure she'd gotten the rental car okay. Supposedly I was in Talkeetna "taking care of business."

When his phone rang, Charlie handed it to Heather, saying I was calling for her. We chatted for a moment as I spied on her from a few yards away.

"Honey, we'll be together in just a little while once you get here to Talkeetna," I fibbed. "You're going to love this little town, and I can't wait to see you." I saw her scanning the baggage carousel, looking for her luggage and smiling as she talked with me.

"I can't wait to see you, either." Heather's voice carried all of the emotion of our time apart, and I couldn't tease her any longer.

"Well, then, why don't you turn around?"

She pivoted and saw me right away, all smiles with a three-week beard and several pounds lighter, but of course she recognized me and rushed over. I stood and took a few steps toward her, but she was in my arms in a flash. (Later, she told me my prank was the most romantic thing that had ever happened to her.) We drove back to Talkeetna, tired but content. We jabbered about the climb, but mostly I stared at Heather. I hadn't forgotten, yet I had somehow tucked away my memory of how beautiful she was, and it was as if I was discovering her all over again. Heather and I spent a few days in town, staying at the Roadhouse and wandering into all the shops. We also took a grand flight around Denali—how spectacular it was to fly around the summit and share that view with her! We spent another couple of days visiting Denali National Park, viewing "the great one" from the far distance.

In one of the shops, we spotted this pretty little gold pendant in the shape of a whale's tale. In Inuit culture, this representation of an animal crucial to their survival shows respect for their prey. Like many indigenous people, the native Alaskans honor the hunted; in fact, the hunting is itself a way of demonstrating respect, an avenue to food sharing and important whaling rituals.[8] In some ways, this attitude toward the whale mirrors my attitude toward the mountain: irreverence for its power amounts to blasphemy; taking for granted any outing on one of these great mountains invites the wrath of the mountain gods. *Peak bagging*, the pursuit of climbing with the aim only of securing bragging rights, strikes me as vulgar. But climbing with the intention of learning, admiring, and sharing can be a good and decent pursuit, even noble.

So the whale tail is meaningful in that way. This particular piece of jewelry was also unusual in that it depicted the Raven *(Yéil)* and Eagle *(Cha'ak)*, their heads and beaks forming the flukes of the tail. These spirit animals figure prominently in creation stories told by the Alaskan Tlingit and Haida clans, and each clan further identifies people within it with either the Raven or the Eagle, and (the shopkeeper told me) the two are allowed to intermarry. I considered the pendant a symbol of good luck and bought it for Heather, telling her that it also represented the two of us coming together, the bond we shared. It felt as if this trinket were summing up so many things: Heather's return to Alaska, my return to high altitude, our deepening love, and the promise of future adventures as yet unknown.

5
ALTITUDE

IN THE LATE NINETIES, mountaineer Alex Abramov earned acclaim for perching a Land Rover atop an 18,510-foot volcano in Russia. The feat began with Alex and his team driving without incident to just above 9,000 feet, but then it morphed into an epic struggle with tire chains, winches, several breakdowns, and multiple repairs. It ended after forty-three days with the thing at the top of the dome of Mount Elbrus, where the ten men drove a few victory laps in the ice and snow, unconcerned that there might be an eruption because the volcano had been dormant for more than two thousand years.

Pleased with themselves, they left the Land Rover where it was and retreated to the Black Sea to relax for a couple of weeks. When they returned to collect their property, the descent turned out to be much hairier than the way up, though substantially quicker, with the vehicle tumbling ass over teakettle down the volcano. Fortunately, the driver jumped out of the SUV just before it hit a huge rock, but then a tire broke loose and careened toward several members of the team standing nearby, coming at them like a giant bowling ball heading for a set of human ninepins. Miraculously, everyone remained unharmed and walked away needing only a stiff drink. Ultimately, this strange achievement put them in the 1997 Guinness Book of World Records for the highest vehicular-assisted mountain climb.[1]

Alex told me this story while we were sitting at base camp on Mount Everest in May of 2004, just three weeks after I'd read about him online. I'd been making plans for my own trip to Mount Elbrus (on foot, sans Land Rover), but I set that aside when I stumbled onto something more exciting that Alex had planned. His website said he would take a couple of people with his Russian adventure team to Mount Everest, assuming the outsiders' resumes were acceptable and they could fork over $10,000. Knowing a bargain, I couldn't pick up the phone fast enough.

"Hallo?" Alex sounded a bit like Boris Badenov from *The Rocky and Bullwinkle Show*, but he was all business. When he asked me about my athletic history, I gave him the broad strokes, including my ultrarunning records and firsts, as well as my exploits in multiday adventure racing, both of which had laid the groundwork for serious mountaineering. I can't say he was impressed, but it sounded as if he'd accept me after only a few minutes' conversation.

Still, I told him that I had dreamed of climbing the world's tallest mountain since childhood, and I'd been actively preparing for it for more than twenty years, gradually increasing the distances I covered on foot, continuing to challenge myself on steep climbs, and gaining the technical skill to handle the gear and deal with emergencies. At the age of fifty-two, I considered mountain climbing a privilege and didn't take the summit for granted, I explained. Experiences on Denali in 2002 had given me the confidence to go after more challenging ascents, and in 2003, I'd climbed in the Andes on Aconcagua, the world's highest mountain outside of Asia. For our honeymoon later that year, my wife Heather and I had reached the top of Africa's highest peak, Kilimanjaro.

I asked all kinds of questions about logistics and what services, exactly, his team would provide. Satisfied with his answers and enjoying his dry wit, I popped the question.

"I want to climb Mount Everest with you. Will you have me?"

"One spot open, sure," he agreed. "You send money right away."

I have no idea if there really was only one spot left or if this was simply a sales tactic. No doubt he was pleased that I could pay in U.S. dollars, which were strong against the ruble. The $10,000 would cover climbing costs, including a couple bottles of oxygen. Alex's crew would pitch tents and cook for everyone at Base Camp (BC) at seventeen thousand feet and Advanced Base Camp (ABC) at twenty-one thousand feet, and above that, they would set up tents, and we'd be responsible for hauling our cooking gear, food, sleeping bags and pads, a bottle of oxygen, and anything else we chose to bring. Alex would also introduce me to a Sherpa if I wanted someone to guide me all the way to the top, but that would incur an additional cost paid to Alex, and I'd tip the Sherpa directly, as well.

Without hesitation, I sent him a cashier's check as a deposit. There wasn't much time to prepare, as the team would gather in less than a month. I didn't worry about that, though, since my base fitness level was already excellent, carried over from years of running and climbing, and Heather and I were living in St. Mary's, Colorado, at 10,400 feet, so two or three times a week I was in the habit of heading nine miles down the road and running back up again, gaining about three thousand feet in that relatively short distance. *I'm as ready as I'll ever be,* I thought.

—————

Great things happen when man meets the mountains.
—Reinhold Messner

WITHIN AN HOUR of my arrival in Kathmandu, I found Alex at the hotel to give him the balance of the money I owed him, and right away, he wanted me to run an errand for him: would I find us a generator? He knew I'd grown up on a farm and was familiar with mechanical things, but he wanted to make sure I could negotiate a good deal. Of course! I'm as frugal as they come, I assured him, plus I'd be able to maintain the generator at base camp, too. Win-win. He sent me off with instructions to locate the generator, get us a good price, then come back and we'd go pay for and pick it up together.

As I walked down the corridor away from his room, something

smelled off. Following my nose, I quickly discovered a string of fish tied up like Tibetan prayer flags at the hotel exit. *That's odd,* I thought. *But, hey, when in Rome.* Later, I found out that this had nothing to do with local customs; the fish belonged to Alex, and the hotel staff had demanded that he take it down because it was stinking up the place.

Once in town, I found what we needed and struck a deal. With my nonexistent Nepali and the salesman's broken English, still we managed to agree that I'd be back to pay and pick it up the next day. When we arrived, Alex wanted to haggle and tried to further lower the price, clearly enjoying the animated back-and-forth. The salesman was unamused, and we wound up paying extra just to convince the fellow to give it to us. So, in my first days with Alex, I made two generalizations about what Russian men enjoy: 1) dried fish, and 2) negotiation.

Back in my own room, which reminded me a little of barracks, I forgot about the overpriced generator and made a journal entry:

April 10, 2004. At the age of five, I sat in front of a black-and-white TV at home in Greeley, Colorado. The images I saw, through the fuzz that was our best reception back then, were of climbers struggling to summit some mountain. I didn't know which mountain, but it didn't matter. A rescue had just taken place, and the fingers and toes of the mountain climbers were severely frostbitten.

This was all a great curiosity to my young mind. Having grown up on a dairy farm on the eastern plains of Colorado, mountain climbing wasn't something I could even imagine, but somehow I connected to them, too. I wanted to be on that mountain. I wanted to see, feel, smell, and hear everything that those climbers were experiencing. I wanted to share the experiences of scaling a big mountain.

Soon after seeing those TV images, I learned about Mount Everest. That it is the tallest mountain in the world. I was fascinated. Then and there, I started dreaming of climbing that high mountain....

Sitting in the comfort of the hotel, my mind wanders back to [that time]. I remember commandeering a straw stack to make my own little world: building tunnels with tent-like rooms within the bales and scrambling up the sides of the stack, pretending it was that great mountain! Somehow, those feelings never subsided. So here I am again, not only on a metaphysical level, but on a physical one, ready to attempt climbing that great mountain. It's good to be here after more than 45 years of waiting and dreaming.

It was finally time, the fulfillment of a childhood dream.

It felt as if the mountaineers I'd revered since childhood were present, all around me. I imagined them walking down the street to the Rum Doodle Bar and Restaurant, where I was excited to see their autographs on the walls. The place is significant in certain circles, as mountain climbers have been imbibing there since before Edmund Hillary and Tenzing Norgay first summited Everest on May 29, 1953. Climbing paraphernalia and signatures decorate the place; more than six hundred people who have climbed to the top also held pen in hand and leaned against the beige walls to leave their mark there, including some of the most famous, such as Hillary, and many others who became the first to summit under extraordinary conditions, such as using no supplemental oxygen (Reinhold Messner and Peter Habeler), or first ascents via the different routes. Some signatures are under glass.

No one can sign without first proving they're worthy by showing photos of themselves at the top, getting corroborating eyewitness accounts, and passing muster with Elizabeth Hawley, who is considered the "keeper of the mountains." An accomplished journalist born in 1923, Hawley moved to Nepal in the early 1960s and never left, thereafter keeping careful records on the Himalayan expeditions. As of this writing, she has tallied 7,646 summits of Everest by 4,469 people; the Nepalese have made 4,863 of those summits and foreigners have made 2,783. She has also kept the death toll: from 1924 to 2017, they totaled 288, of whom seventy died on the way *down*.

Standing there, I imagined that I might sign the wall, too. Bonus: summiteers earn the restaurant's membership card, entitling them to free food at the Rum Doodle for the rest of their lives.

THE NIGHT before we left Kathmandu to begin acclimation on Mount Everest, I arranged my thoughts and visualized the climb, something I expected to do repeatedly once we were underway. I considered it part of a "programming" process to clear my mind of anything that might interfere with the focus I'd require. In the past, I'd done this for other difficult pursuits and found it helpful in big-mountain climbs. On this day, I imagined the sights and sounds of the vibrant city fading away, the bicycle bells and truck horns, the shopping and bargaining, the men wearing gray and black, and the women in colorful dresses and tops growing more distant as the countryside becoming my new reality.

I can't think of any major endeavor where I haven't practiced this kind of mental preparation, just like many other people who want to maximize their performance. Visualization isn't just new-age puffery. It has very real effects; stories about and studies of its power abound. One fellow imprisoned in the USSR for spying played mental chess with himself while in solitary confinement, intending to use this time to become the best in the world. In fact, after he was released, Natan Sharansky beat the world champion Garry Kasparov in 1996. Research on brain patterns shows that they are essentially the same whether athletes are actively participating in their sport or simply imagining it, and one study showed that virtual workouts yielded half the muscle gain as actual weightlifting.

The best results, of course, are achieved when you can do both: imagine your success as well as pursue it in the real world. Gymnasts practice mentally while injured and return to competition more skilled than ever. Champion golfers and tennis players swear by this technique to enhance their game and build their confidence. Soccer players find out in advance which uniform they'll wear during the match so they can vividly picture themselves, the field, and the victory. Muhammad Ali, Mary Lou Retton, Michael Phelps, Tiger Woods, Jack Nicklaus, Venus Williams, and so many more stellar athletes employ their imagination in service of honing their skills. As Albert Einstein observed, "Imagination is more important than science." With my own experience plus all that evidence and a genius's endorsement to boot, I'm inclined to agree.

WE DROVE to Base Camp on April 13, 2004, and stayed there for a week, setting up camp, reviewing logistics, getting to know each other, and going for day hikes to acclimate. When we were ready to move on to Advance Base Camp, we started the day with an early breakfast, and then the monk arrived from nearby Rongbuk Monastery to perform *puja* with us. During the ceremony, authentic prayer flags attached to a pole on the hill just above our camp fluttered in the breeze with the clear blue sky and Everest as the backdrop. Just below the flagpole, the monks placed a firebox stocked with small branches, and below that was a platform of stones where we laid objects to be blessed. Mine included the necklace I'd bought for Heather in Alaska, one that she'd worn every day except when I was racing or climbing. Then, and only then, would she take it off and give it to me as a reminder of home as I kept it and her close to my heart.

I also put a banner on the stones, one I intended to take to the top of the world. The banner represented the Religious Teachers Filippini, a charity I had been involved with for a few years and that had provided motivation to me during particularly tough tests of physical endurance. As the monk chanted prayers, he intermittently tossed rice and corn flour into the air, rang a bell, and twisted a drumlike instrument with a ball attached that would beat on one side, then the other. During the ritual, ravens and crows flew overhead and landed within forty feet of the ceremonial site. Sometimes superstitious, I interpreted this as a good sign, and I also took some of the rice that the monk blessed for our use, planning to throw it in the air on the second step of the mountain, a notoriously sketchy spot.

After *puja*, we took a team photo then got busy packing our supplies and equipment into sacks and barrels.

We carefully weighed and balanced everything, lashing up to 150 pounds to each yak outfitted with a wooden yoke. Though modest in size (up to six hundred pounds), these great fuzzy beasts were lean and strong, each wearing a woolen knit collar and hand-hammered metal bell the herders had given them, each bell with a unique sound to identify the individual animal. They reminded me of the Holstein cattle my family had tended on our dairy farm while I was growing up. The sounds and the smell, particularly, were reminiscent—the plodding of hooves over ground, their mooing, and the scent of grazing herbivores was familiar and calming. I watched the herders pack grass on some of the yaks' backs for all of them to eat and was amazed at how little they would need. They were compact and solid as any animal I've been around, and draped in long hair that covered their entire bodies.

The Russian Adventure team at Everest base camp, Tibet, 2004, including team leader Alex Abromov (standing, second from l), me (kneeling, first on the l), and the only other American, David D'Angelo (seated, far r).

After we were done with the yaks, I had a little time before our departure, so I went for a walk. About four and a half miles below the camp, I reached the monastery, passing about 150 off-duty yaks grazing and resting beside the huge hills. Many of the monks there delighted in practicing their English on me, showed me around, and wished me well, telling me *go slowly, slowly* as they motioned to the top of the great mountain.

Good advice. I found that, over the coming days, I had to make my peace with how slowly everything, including me, proceeded. The weather was the greatest factor; if it was clear, we could consider moving on, and if it was bleak, so were our prospects for progress. One night, a jet stream had entered the area above 24,600 feet and could be heard throughout the night, keeping everyone below awake and somewhat on edge. Prayer flags strung throughout the camp fluttered horizontally, and the tent flies and doors, if not secured, flapped violently. *How long before these tents are in tatters?* I wondered.

So we learned to be patient, to wait out the weather, and use the time to our advantage in getting accustomed to the altitude, and to do our best to deal with the inevitable boredom that comes with idleness. I struggled with all of it, longing for my family, and feeling frustrated when I couldn't contact them. And then, just when I'd think I was about to lose my mind, I'd get up to climb out of the tent and then, like clockwork—*zzzzzz!*— the zipper stuck. I had to spend the next little while teasing the teeth back into alignment, wiggling the slider until the chain came back together and I could get the thing undone and get myself out of the tent, exasperated and out of breath. At one point, I gave up on the back door zipper and sewed it shut, leaving the main entry the only way out. Zippers gained a mystical significance for me—they were powerful reminders to stay in the moment, to deal calmly with the reality of now, to improvise with whatever's handy, to let any fixation on what wasn't immediately present (climbing, contact with family, other things I considered a more constructive use of my time) vanish into the thin air.

To aid in acclimation, we trekked back and forth between Base Camp (about seventeen thousand feet) and Advance Base Camp (about twenty-one thousand feet) three times in as many weeks, then finally pressed on to Camp 1 (only slightly higher in elevation, close to twenty-three thousand feet) on May 7. At that stage, I settled into the routine, growing philosophical about, well, everything: zippers, wind, sleeplessness (and weird dreams when I could finally nod off), the extreme cold, the warmth of my sleeping bag, the loss of energy and inability to recover at that altitude, you name it. As we left Advance Base Camp for the final summit push, I wrote in my journal:

> *This is an excellent training ground for control freaks of the world. It will reduce you to a more realistic state, the one in which I'm striving to live. Things up here test you. They are what they are, and if you cannot accept the conditions that exist, there's only one path—and it leads down into the comfort level of lower ground. For some, I guess staying in or quickly hurrying back to that*

comfort level is all right, but I do believe stepping out of that comfort zone is
where valuable lessons can be learned.

The mountain teaches you to adapt. To adjust. To pay attention to
the environment and pay it the proper deference. To go slowly, indeed.

The people who live near *Chomolongma* work the land and revere
the mountain, giving it a holy reverence most Westerners don't. I can't
imagine any one of them thinking about "conquering" the summit or
"bagging" the peak; the idea of overpowering such majesty would be
both foolish and impious. Instead, they experience a connection with
the "Goddess Mother of the World." In establishing my own relationship with Everest, I felt an ancient energy as powerful as it is enormous; it made me feel humbled and thankful to be in that place in that
precise point in time, realizing that it would never happen again in
exactly the same way.

In no way do I think I'm the lone American who experiences such
things; even government agencies attempt to translate this metaphysical connectedness into practical actions—environmental stewardship.
In the 1970s, for example, the U.S. Forest Service, Bureau of Land
Management, and National Park Service all recognized the need for
some kind of educational program, and they began a movement to
instill "wilderness ethics" among those who enjoy the outdoors. This
gave rise to a slogan every Boy Scout knows: *leave no trace.* The idea is
that you enter, enjoy, and exit a place without disrupting, damaging, or
disturbing it in any way. This means that if you're in wilderness, you
don't leave so much as a gum wrapper or even a footprint behind. We
can extend this to visiting other cultures: "leave no trace" could mean
that you do your best not to diminish or, at the very least, offend
anyone. At best, you gently assimilate, embracing what you can. It is its
own kind of acclimation: you adjust to the place where you are, not the
other way around.

On May 25, 2004, I did reach the top of the world. I summited
Mount Everest with my friend David (the only other American in our
group—a younger man with a great attitude who kept me in stitches
and called me "Pop") and with the assistance of Sherpa Pemba, who
was indispensable. At the start, the expedition had three Sherpas and

as we prepared for the trip that would lead us up and over major Himalayan passes from the south to the north side of Everest. I told Alex that, although I had paid for one of the Sherpas, I would let the expedition use whomever that Sherpa would be, along with the other two (as they were short on Sherpas) and then I would choose one Sherpa for the final summit push that would be a few days in length. That way I could watch the Sherpas and pick the one that I could get along with and was the most impressed with.

After a couple of weeks on the mountains watching the Sherpas doing carries up to the higher camps, I knew Pemba was the man for me. He was superbly fit and strong and always smiling. About five foot five inches tall and 155 pounds, he was the consummate athlete. He always pitched in, and was always willing to help out the expedition in any way he could. During the summit push, he met me at the 21,000-foot high camp and we spent the next three days heading up the hill. His job was to make sure I was on track, and that the tents at the higher camps were upright and habitable. He made sure on the last day that I didn't get lost. He also carried one extra oxygen bottle for me.

The climb itself was unremarkable by the standard of other harrowing tales of Everest; most famously, Jon Krakauer's *Into Thin Air* captured the level of disaster that can occur up there as you approach the death zone. Our ascent was nothing like that. Despite temperatures regularly well below zero, winds that whipped at thirty or more miles per hour, and intense claustrophobia, the worst thing that happened to me was falling into a rushing glacial stream, which could have ended my life—as I stretched my arms around a rock to stop my fall, I imagined with chagrin my hometown paper's headline: "Local Man First to Drown on Mount Everest!"—but it ended all right, with a damn cold trek up to ABC, but me feeling no worse for wear, aside from having been scared out of my wits. (Well, that, and having to smell a tent mate's feet all the time, as we slept head to toe, but then, I didn't have the same misfortune David did, accidentally drinking his own urine during the night.) I lost weight and killed a few brain cells, but for the most part returned intact to my wife and family.

More seriously, there were a half dozen people who died while I was on Everest, not a record, but tragic nonetheless. Two of the people were climbers from Bulgaria who were climbing without oxygen and died, overcome by the elements. This scared me because I had gotten to know them a bit, and befriended them. Although others' deaths were sobering, to be sure, they had seemed somewhat unreal, and I had been able to dissociate from any fear I might have felt. I had become so vested in climbing the mountain that I simply set aside any unpleasant facts of our expedition, including death, and tried not to think about them so I could instead focus on the task at hand. When I did think of them, it was obliquely: I cast their stories as a kind of cautionary tale, and reminded myself to always keep safety in the fore of my mind.

Sometimes, though, it was impossible to deny the horror of what had happened. On my way up, I passed the body of Tsewang Paljor, commonly referred to as Green Boots, which is used as a landmark, a morbid sort of directional signage indicating where you turn right up the ridge. I still vividly remember seeing and stepping around the young Bulgarian who was forever entombed in his red and yellow climbing suit. (Alex and the other Bulgarian climbers asked me to take a picture of his face to verify insurance claims, but I refused and let him rest in peace.) For a long while after I returned home, whenever I saw those colors even from the corner of my eye, it took me back to the mountain and that horrible moment.

In comparison, though, our expedition wasn't nearly the tragedy many others have experienced. And since then, I've come to wonder if anyone should be climbing this mountain anymore. It is difficult, and rewarding, and remarkable, and humbling—but is it worth it?

Not long ago, I read an account of what happened to Paljor by Rachel Nuwer, who visited his home nearly a decade after I spotted his remains on Everest.[2] She began the story with an epigraph, a 1924 quote from George Mallory: "It is clear that the stake [the mountaineer] risks to lose is a great one with him: it is a matter of life and death.... To win the game he has first to reach the mountain's summit —but further, he has to descend in safety. The more difficult the way and the more numerous the dangers, the greater is his victory." It's apt, as we know Paljor died on the way down, if not much else about why he perished.

Nuwer's conversations with the man's mother revealed, though, that he had spun a story about climbing a mountain, and only later had she discovered it was the highest mountain in the world. We do also know that on the day Paljor summited, things started out bad and got worse. Despite dangerous conditions, he ascended with a couple of comrades (another went down), and that was the last anyone saw of Paljor until they discovered his corpse with his feet, clad in neon green boots, still on the pathway so that climbers have to step over his legs.

The mountain gods did not smile on Paljor, nor on hundreds of other climbers, and I look back and think how easily that could have been me frozen on that mountainside. It also makes me reflect and ask, what about ethics on Mount Everest? What is the protocol for rescue? (Some say that there were climbers who came upon Paljor in his distress and, later, death throes, and did nothing for him.) I agree that there are risks involved climbing there, and once a person steps foot on that or any mountain, the responsibility for staying safe is entirely their own. Don't expect a rescue, as it may risk other people's lives, and it is all part of knowing your limits and then, God forbid, if something goes wrong, you are on your own and don't have a choice other than to accept your fate, whatever that might be. I got lucky. As I say, the mountains don't care, and sometimes people can do no more than the mountain.

A VIOLENT EARTHQUAKE measuring 7.8 on the Richter scale hit Nepal on April 25, 2015, killing more than nine thousand people and injuring an estimated twenty-three thousand more. Ancient buildings crumbled, and entire villages were crushed. The quake triggered an avalanche on Mount Everest, killing nineteen people there. While the loss on the mountain seems insignificant compared to the incredible damage done in the surrounding area, the number of lives lost make it the deadliest day on Mount Everest. In 2015, for the first time in forty-one years, no one reached the top of the mountain, as the avalanches closed down commercial expeditions for the rest of the climbing season.[3]

Even as it has become "easier" to climb—due to plenty of companies offering to guide people on climbs with fixed ropes and plenty of supplemental oxygen plus the local Nepalese, the Sherpas, to safeguard and shuttle them to the top—Mount Everest has somehow become more dangerous. Since the 1990s, just about anybody with means has been allowed on the mountain (in 2015, companies charged between $30,000 and $100,000 per person[4]), although for a while, the more experienced climbers viewed this with great suspicion and, in some cases, derision. In 2003, when Sir Edmund Hillary marked the passing of fifty years since he and Tenzing Norgay were the first to summit there, he counseled that the government should withhold climbing permits for a few years to let it recover from the onslaught of what amounts to tourists.[5] Reinhold Messner, who was the first along with Peter Habeler to summit without supplemental oxygen in 1978, dismissed the high numbers of "trophy hunters" who merely entertained an interest in a fashionable mountain, and he lamented that Everest has been reduced to a "consumable."[6]

Call me superstitious, but I've come to believe that disregard and disrespect have plucked the mountain gods' last nerves. I agree with Hillary: give the mountain a break. It's been trampled enough. Humans quite literally leave their shit laying all around up there—not only their climbing trash, but also their body waste. In addition, about half don't have the skills or experience to climb in such an extreme environment, thus endangering the lives of others, particularly the Sherpas; some days, the ascent is made like pack mules, nose to butt, in a long if colorful train of down-swaddled sightseers. Of necessity, when people die, they are left where they fall. If you imagine Everest as a vast expanse of glistening ice and uncluttered beauty (much like Denali), you have it wrong. Seeing it might actually make you gag; *The Washington Post* described Everest as a "fecal time bomb."[7]

If you're not on board with my mountain-gods theory, consider the undeniable human toll on Mount Everest. It's a morbid trade-off where no one wins; in addition to other duties, Sherpas do incredibly dangerous prep work to make it easier for people who pay them to go from eighteen thousand to above twenty thousand feet quickly, as this is where avalanches are most likely to occur.

The Sherpas, like (l to r) Tenzing, Dorje, and Pemba. are the true mountaineers.

Not coincidentally, avalanches are the leading cause of death for Sherpas who die on the mountain. Where are their paying customers hurrying to go? Ironically, it's to the "death zone" and on to the summit. This area above twenty-six thousand feet is where the inexperienced—not the Sherpas—are most likely to fall or to overestimate their stamina.[8] If you are ill-prepared but pay for the pleasure of reaching the roof of the world, you can quite literally rush to your death.

I do think that the locals have a respect for the mountain that most others who climb don't. To me, it is a sacred quest; at least, that is how I looked at it while I was climbing. To race up the mountain with disregard to everything it has to offer—peace, beauty, wonder, joy, immense spiritual presence—is to miss the point of climbing. Is the mountain being overused and taken for granted? After hearing all that has gone on the past couple of years, I would say yes.

I'm not one to believe that the mountain needs some sort of human sacrifice to avenge (there are those who do believe that), but I do believe we have to be stewards of Everest and do what we know to be right, as what we do on and for the mountain reflects the same for us and who we are. Sure, I may be projecting feelings on the mountain, but how we are trudging up that mountain seems to yield nothing but a false sense of accomplishment. Even George Mallory, when asked what's the use of climbing Mount Everest, replied, "It's no use."

Clearly, climbing Mount Everest isn't for everyone. I'm not even sure it's for anyone anymore, although people were allowed to go up again just a year after that devastating earthquake. Yes, my 2004 ascent was the culmination of a dream. Do I regret it? No. Knowing what I know now, would I make the same choice? I'm not so sure. At the time, my daughter Elaine protested loudly, pronounced my plans selfish, and all but called me stupid for risking my life. Today, I can acknowledge she was right.

Consider the rest of what Mallory had to say about it to the *New York Times:*

> There is not the slightest prospect of any gain whatsoever. Oh, we may learn a little about the behavior of the human body at high altitudes, and possibly medical men may turn our observation to some account for the purposes of aviation. But otherwise nothing will come of it. We shall not bring back a single bit of gold or silver, not a gem, nor any coal or iron. We shall not find a single foot of earth that can be planted with crops to raise food. It's no use. So, if you cannot understand that there is something in man which responds to the challenge of this mountain and goes out to meet it, that the struggle is the struggle of life itself upward and forever upward, then you won't see why we go. What we get from this adventure is just sheer joy. And joy is, after all, the end of life. We do not live to eat and make money. We eat and make money to be able to enjoy life. That is what life means and what life is for.

So, yes, I still believe that climbing Everest (at least a metaphorical one) is a worthy pursuit.

Werner Herzog, the filmmaker who documented one of Messner's freestyle climbs of K4 and K5, reportedly once said, "I particularly loathe pseudo-adventurism, where the mountain climb becomes about exploring your personal limits."[9] Really? I call bullshit, unless that is *all* it's about without regard to how your actions affect others, including your loved ones and, certainly, the place where you'll undertake such a journey. Can I do this and "leave no trace"? Can I intelligently assess risk and prepare in such a way that it is minimized?

It's something that I did, too, saying I was exploring the limits of human endurance, which is a selfish way of saying I'm going to prove to myself and others that I can do this while disregarding those who have to endure the pain of my absence. For them, it is a struggle to survive also, but they are left with thoughts of why someone would go and put themselves in peril by choice. I question this myself, wondering why it is that I have to do these extreme events. Is it to fill a void in myself, or do I view myself so inadequate that I have to prove myself? Am I comfortable in my own skin? I suggest that some risks are worth taking and some not, but to discover the why of taking an unacceptable risk sometimes remains a mystery.

PART III

FIRE

FANNING FLAMES

What matters most is how well you walk through the fire.
—Charles Bukowski, poet

6

PERSEVERANCE

THOUGH I'VE EXPLORED the world by climbing mountains and scaling rock walls, crossing ice fields and the tundra, paddling on streams, rivers, and oceans, no other place has so completely captured my imagination as the desert: Death Valley, in particular. Having covered thousands of miles on foot there, I respect and even relish its intense heat, which has scorched a landscape shaped by wind into soft dunes and striated rock faces.

In the summer, muted earth tones—tans, browns, oranges, reds, and drab greens—paint the horizon, meeting the blue sky in a far-off seam of color. Yet many miles collapse into just a few in the mind's eye, making distant landmarks seem deceptively close, and bringing mirages shimmering to life. On a solitary road winding through the valley, several abrupt climbs interrupt long, nearly flat stretches of asphalt. Both plants and animals display rugged strength. Creosote, cactus, and desert holly poke through the shifting desert floor. During a rare breeze or, more commonly, a hot wind and sandstorm, resolute groves of Joshua trees stand stiff and nearly unmoving. On occasion, you can hear a coyote pack howl, catch scorpions scurrying along the roadside, or glimpse bats flapping overhead. At night, the sky glimmers, lit only by the stars.

Death Valley is the hottest place on earth, the driest part of North America, and although this land has been called alien and strange, I've never felt as much at home as I do there. The place intoxicates. It punishes. It purifies.

Of course, I'm not alone in my deep connection to this desert. The Timbisha Shoshone Tribe have made it their home for centuries, hunting and harvesting, most of them spending the cooler months in the depths of the valley and the warmer ones up higher, near and on places like Telescope Peak. Outsiders began to arrive in the mid-1800s, and the land bustled with mining operations procuring gold, silver, and borax. By the turn of the century, however, companies like the Harmony Borax Works had boomed then busted there, flourishing and then disappearing somewhat mysteriously.

Later in 1922, the con man Walter Scott convinced millionaire Albert Mussey Johnson to invest in a gold mine and build a winter home in northern Death Valley. Even after Johnson and his wife discovered that the mine deal was a fraud, they still enjoyed Scotty's company and returned regularly to Death Valley to continue building their two-story villa. Due to a surveying mistake, the Johnson's home was built on government land, and once this error was realized, construction halted, and the Johnson family never completely finished the project. Years later, the National Park Service acquired the villa and opened it as a tourist attraction, which is now known as Scotty's Castle (FYI: not a castle).

More recently, Death Valley became a proving ground for adventurers and athletes. In 1966, Jean-Pierre Marquant made the first summer crossing there, going 102 miles in nine days. In October 1969, two friends from San Diego, Jim Burnworth and Stan Rodefer, went even farther, hiking nearly 150 miles from the depths of the Badwater Basin across Death Valley and on to the top of nearby Mount Whitney. They took two weeks to go from this lowest point in North America (282 feet below sea level) to this highest summit in the contiguous United States (14,505 feet). Burnworth and Rodefer crossed the salt flats and then took a direct route to the mountain trail, forgoing paved roads, which surely made their path more difficult and dangerous.

Theirs was the first "Lowest/Highest" hike on record, documented in some detail by the park rangers and reported in an article printed in the *San Diego Tribune* ("Hikers View High, Low Sites in the U.S.," November 4, 1969). The men had no idea they were doing anything unique and, evidently, had embarked on the trip "just for the heck of it." According to Rodefer's daughter, they were sustained on food and water they'd buried in the desert beforehand and slept under the stars all but one night, when they took shelter in a defunct mine shaft where they discovered an old box of dynamite.[1]

A year later, a Brit named Ken Crutchlow put an ad in San Francisco newspapers challenging anyone to race him in Death Valley. A badass adventurer and, frankly, a trouble-seeker from way back (he once stowed away on a German luxury liner), he asserted that "only mad dogs and Englishmen go out in the noonday sun," so it was unlikely to find any "rebellious colonists [who] would have what it takes to complete the race." He did find one somewhat foolhardy taker, Bruce Maxwell. The two set out to conquer the desert in the summer of 1970:

> Neither man had ever been to Death Valley or had any idea what he was getting himself into, but Crutchlow seemed determined to make the contest perversely difficult. Not only did he want to race for 134 miles, essentially the entire length of the valley, he insisted on doing so in early August, when the basin assuredly would be roasting.... "Why try to avoid the very thing that gave the place its name?" he scoffed....
>
> [Crutchlow] began, as he had begun many of his athletic endeavors, decked out in a pin-striped suit and bowler, and with an umbrella tucked under his arm. Once out of sight of the media, he changed into more traditional running clothes.[2]

Both men battled on, with Crutchlow bungling a turn and losing three hours to get back on course, and suffered greatly in the heat, but ultimately completed their 134-mile course in five days. Maxwell edged out Crutchlow by just six hours.

In early August of 1977, another man succeeded in making it across Death Valley, adding the ascent of Mount Whitney just as Burnworth and Rodefer had done, and he went the entire 146 miles in less than four days (84 hours). Al Arnold stayed on the road from Badwater Basin then turned onto Highway 190, crossing over three mountain ranges (Amargosa, Panamint, and Coso) and through three arid valleys (Death, Panamint, and Owens), and then went up the trail to the summit. This was Arnold's third attempt to complete the grueling course he'd set for himself, which some considered an impossible feat. He was a forty-seven-year-old health club director[3] who had once weighed three hundred pounds but gotten himself in condition to compete in the 1968 U.S. Masters Track & Field Championships, then committed himself to long-term health and fitness. Search online, and you'll quickly discover photos of Al running in tighty-whities, which reveal his toughened body.

Reflecting on his Badwater-to-Whitney-summit experience years later, he writes:

...it never occurred to me of being anything other than "an extension of the environment!" Many individuals have died on these desert floors, and I'm sure that it wasn't an easy way to die!! All ULTRAS that dare accept the challenge of traversing these hazards of Mother Nature, do so within Her "natural guidelines." ... How lucky, it was for me, @30 years ago, to "try again and again", not to have any adversarial conflicts! Other than good old Mother Nature. She spanked me very hard![4]

Spanked may be too kind a word. Not only is 146 miles a long way to go, but Death Valley posts the hottest temperatures of any place on earth. Air temperatures commonly reach the 120s, and it's not unheard of for them to spike 130°F or more. By contrast, they can drop to below freezing at the top of Mount Whitney, even in the middle of summer. What's more, the elevation change over this course is about nineteen thousand feet, with the final twenty-plus miles nearly entirely uphill at a steep grade. Al's previous two failed attempts had taught him to run slower so that the desert wouldn't burn him out before he reached the mountain, to dress head to toe in all white to protect himself during the most blazing hours of sun, to have warmer clothes for the final climb, and to ensure he had enough water, and salt, and sugar. So someone trailed him, driving a support car, to give him the things he needed, but he really made this effort alone. No pacer. No earbuds (they weren't even invented yet). Very little rest. Nothing but Al, the road, and the distance. His effort was pioneering, a break-through in the sport of ultrarunning.

Others attempted to beat his time, but failed to complete the course, much less set a record on it. In 1981, however, a thirty-six-year-old biology teacher and marathoner got the job done in seventy-four hours and thirty-five minutes. Victorious yet humble, Jay Birmingham reported, "The highest temperature was over 120. But it was snowing on the summit of Whitney. This was, without doubt, the toughest 146 miles I've ever run."[5]

After that, though, a handful of runners no longer considered it impossible. On the ten-year anniversary of Al Arnold's finish, five athletes turned the Badwater-to-Whitney-summit course into a race. A pair of Americans faced off against a pair of Brits on July 31, 1987, and a journalist tagged along to cover the contest. Eleanor Adams prevailed, making it to the summit in 53:03, establishing a new course record, setting the bar for both men and women to reach. Alas, her teammate Ken Crutchlow[6] (sans bowler hat and pinstripe suit) reached the top in 126:30 with his pal, the reporter Dave Bolling. So the American team, Jean Ennis and Tom Crawford, won bragging rights with finish times of 58:57 each, even after having gotten caught in a hailstorm on their way up Mount Whitney.[7]

This informal competition and, no doubt, the colorful history of previous crossings, sparked the first official race across Death Valley, held in 1988. Sponsored by an outdoor clothing and gear company, it was dubbed the Hi-Tec Badwater 146, and eight individuals partici-pated by invitation. It was a fairly low-budget enterprise designed to help Hi-Tec break into the sizeable and growing running market, posi-tioning it as a shoe company for ultrarunners. They saw this new venture as a development event, a way both to research product design and to connect with consumers who already had a love for and under-standing of the demands of the outdoors.[8]

This is where the Badwater-to-Whitney race and my story begin to converge. In May 1988, I had entered a twenty-four-hour race in a

Buffalo, New York park, where I ran on a one-mile loop for twenty-four hours straight and was surprised to win it, finishing 122 miles. You read that right: I ran around in circles all day and night.

I went on to place toward the front of the pack at both the Western States that June and the Leadville Trail 100 in August. And then came a September surprise: the silver medal at the twenty-four-hour National Championships with a total of 133 miles. My performance kept improving as I ran farther, and I thought I might have found my talent: I could keep going hard when most other people were reaching the end of their endurance.

Along about then, I read an article by *Runner's World* editor Bart Yasso, who described a "crazy" 146-mile race across Death Valley. His editors had gotten him an invitation in 1989 and, as someone who had previously run, at most, a standard marathon distance of 26.2 miles, Yasso bemoaned his lack of preparation for what he'd encountered there: daytime temperatures that evaporated the sweat off his back before it could moisten his shirt; an overall change of more than nineteen thousand feet, with 14,700 feet of that in elevation gain; and doubtless the most daunting of all, a distance equaling five and a half marathons, 146 miles with the majority of the final "marathon" going uphill at an intimidating grade.

The two-year-old race had few starters that year; of the fifty who had applied, fewer than twenty had been invited to compete, and just Yasso and five others toed the line:

> ...forty-six-year-old female twins who carried resumes to pass out to spectators along the way; Jim Walker, who had dropped out of the race in 1988 after completing 96 miles; Adrian Crane, who carried a modified set of skis on his back, part of a plan to ski across the salt flats and shave twenty miles from the course; and Tom Possert, who'd finished first the year before but was disqualified for unlawful assistance on the course (his crew was photographed dragging him up Whitney). As to why race officials let him participate again, I can only surmise that they needed bodies.[9]

Remarkably, all six finished. Yasso wrote about his two-person crew, the competitors, the difficulty, and the course with such good-natured appreciation for all of it—his trademark straightforward and self-deprecating descriptions of people and places—that I was more than intrigued. And maybe Yasso won? Depends on whether you ask him or Possert, I suppose. But, here's what Bart said in his article:

> I began the ascent of Mount Whitney the next morning at sunrise.
> Jane accompanied me on the climb. It was slow going over rock-strewn
> switchbacks and narrow trails. It took us four and a half hours to get
> to the snow-dusted apex, and we arrived around 10:00 a.m., exhausted
> but elated.... We mugged for a few shots, and then race director David
> Pompel, who had spent the night on the mountain, congratulated me
> for being the second to reach the summit. He also told me that the
> first, Crane, had cut the course and was going to be disqualified. Then
> he admitted he didn't have a U.S. Forest Service permit to hold the
> race on Mount Whitney, so he had appointed a fake finish line at the
> trailhead to Whitney (at mile 135). Possert had been the first to reach
> the phony finish, but for some reason stopped there, never venturing
> up the mountain. I had been the third one to reach the trailhead.
> So how did I do? I don't know. I never checked the official results.
> If you have, don't tell me. I like thinking I placed first, second, and
> third in the same race.[10]

Reading the article, I felt the pull of a new ambition. Maybe I could wangle my way into this race, too. I sent a letter and my athletic resume to the organizers, including my most recent achievement: doing the "Last Great Race," which included finishing all of the American hundred-milers in one year (the four oldest, which were called The Grand Slam, plus two more). No one had ever done that before—run six trail races of 100 miles or more, each spaced about three weeks apart—and I hoped it would get me an invitation to run at the Badwater 146.

Meanwhile, the U.S. Forest Service had made it clear to the Hi-Tec race organizers that, for safety and park preservation, the course for the race had to be shortened to stop short of the wilderness area, cutting off the final eleven miles. This meant that the race should no

90 MARSHALL ULRICH

longer officially go to the top of Mount Whitney. Note that I say *should* and *officially*, because pretty much everyone who signed up to do the 1990 race, including me, assumed we'd go to the top. There was no way we were going to stop at the "phony finish" when the idea behind the race was to go from the lowest to highest points in the contiguous forty-eight states.

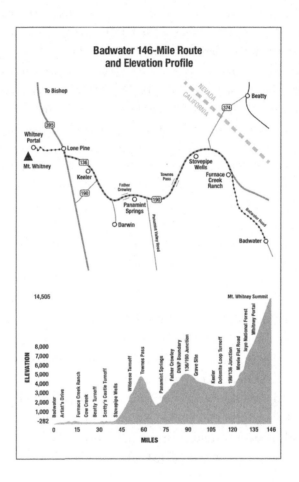

The route established by the 1988 race goes to the Whitney summit.

The first time I ran the race in Death Valley, there were twenty-one starters. Milling around with the other runners before the gun went off, I was excited and confident but scared, too. Everything seemed strange, including the expansive Badwater Basin itself, a salt crust disguising miles of muddy underlayer, which I could see from the starting line. There were so many potential pitfalls, known and unknown, seen and unseen. I wondered, *What will happen?* I'd read about people throwing up (the previous year, Tom Possert had left little piles of half-digested bananas baking on the road), passing out, experiencing both heat stroke *and* hypothermia, and limping to the finish with broken blisters so severe that their feet looked like raw hamburger. Meanwhile, the heat was no joke, hovering around 120 degrees. Before the day of the race, I had explored the first forty miles of the course and also checked the elevation map, which showed the serious incline just up the road from where I stopped. Naively, I was looking forward to that climb, thinking it would bring me relief by lifting me out of the heat.

Hi-Tec conducted a pre-race briefing, and then we all lined up at the start. Right at 6:00 p.m., as the sun hung just above the horizon, we took our first steps down the road and into what felt like a blast furnace. The blacktop radiated heat it had absorbed all day while still more hot air came rushing into the low point of the U.S., careening head on at speeds I'd estimate were near thirty miles per hour. *Welcome to Death Valley, suckers!*

The hot winds didn't let up much. When I arrived at the base of the first climb around 2:00 a.m., the early morning hours brought slightly cooler temperatures, but the wind continued, more like a phalanx of blow dryers than a blast furnace. As I moved up the mountain, I was leading the race, and I made good time going up and over Townes Pass then dropping down into the Panamint Valley before the sun came up again.

As the race went on, daytime temperatures never dropped below 100°F, but I was encouraged. On the second day, sleep-deprived and wearing the same pair of socks and shoes I'd started in, my body suffered some in the heat, but it seemed I was built for this kind of endurance racing. It helped, too, that I wasn't a novice—the race organizers were right to invite only experienced ultrarunners. I had learned the importance of hydration and replacing salt lost through sweat; I wore a white hat with a split tail to protect my neck and shoulders, which had pockets for ice on the top and tails (sounds fancy but it's not); and my crew kept me going with the food I had learned would best sustain me over long distances.

The sights fascinated me when I paid attention to them; I could alternately focus internally as I ran or enjoy my surroundings. We passed through areas with colorful names and gorgeous desert scenery: Dante's Peak and Furnace Creek with the Funeral Mountains in the distance, the Devil's Cornfield where spiky arrowroot plants managed to grow in the dry sand, and Alabama Hills with its lumpy rock formations, prompting the kind of mental play usually reserved for lazy afternoons staring at the clouds. Animal life was scarce, but I did see a lone coyote, a few nighttime bats, and a fair number of scorpions. With this and more to distract and drive me forward, I led for 117 miles, and then Tom caught me, even as I was running at a sub-eight minutes/mile pace. I crossed the road, shook his hand, and told him he was about to beat me fair and square: he was a better man than I.

My two-person support crew, Keith and Priscilla Pippin, were with me the entire distance on the road, leapfrogging the van ahead about every mile or so, giving me water, ice, food, and the occasional pep talk. Each time Keith arrived with a fresh water bottle to exchange for my empty one, he ran alongside me so I wouldn't have to slow down much at all. It was a huge effort on both of their parts. At the end, the three of us felt triumphant just to have gotten to the 135-mile mark in over thirty hours.

At the Whitney Portals (the ostensible finish and the last of the paved road just before starting on the trail to the top of Mt. Whitney), someone told me that Tom had gotten into a disagreement with a Forest ranger.

The ranger had insisted, "You can't have a race in a wilderness area!" But Tom had just continued on, undeterred.

Curious about what was happening, I quietly lurked nearby and saw the race director, Dave Pompel, having it out with the ranger, their conversation escalating to a shouting match. It was a stand-off: the ranger threatened to pull the plug on the race, and Dave didn't have much of an inclination to be intimidated. But then they seemed to reach an agreement: Dave would instruct all the runners to strip off their race numbers, and the ranger would allow us to pass. My impression was that it turned out like a typical divorce settlement with both parties walking away feeling like they had gotten the shaft. About three-quarters of the runners passed through the portals and went up, or tried to go up. Word had trickled down that the race was to stop at the 135-mile mark, but most of us prided ourselves on finishing the "real race." I know I did.

Ultimately, I finished second behind Tom. Of the twenty-one runners who started, seventeen completed the 135 miles to the Whitney Portals, with a handful continuing to the summit, and four did not finish (DNF).

For me, Death Valley and Mount Whitney aren't acquired tastes; I loved them the first time I experienced them. As soon as I finished, I knew I wanted to return. *How fast can I do this race if I run it again? How hard and far can I push myself here?* Back then, I felt that I could do just about anything I set my mind to, so I could hardly wait for the next year. *Will I break the newly set record, which was a little over twenty-eight hours to the portals and just over forty hours to the top?*

Not only had the race stoked my ambition, but never before had I felt so connected to Mother Earth as when I was in the midst of that desert solitude or immersed in the thin mountain air, feeling as if I was breathing the sky. Of course, I applied for the race again, and I was both honored and humbled to be invited back.

That next year, in 1991, I won the Hi-Tec Badwater 146; they persisted in calling it that until at least 1993, despite the shortened official distance. Fourteen started, and fourteen finished; about half continued to the top of Mount Whitney. I set the record for the 146-mile course—just under thirty-four hours—that still stands. Dave Pompel gave me a finisher's silver belt buckle and a $1,000 prize. I went on to win it three more times in 1992, 1993, and 1996.

By 1999, Matt had finally acquiesced some to the park service's demands; the T-shirt I have from that year says, "Hi-Tec Badwater '99: 135 foot blistering, knee pounding, joint punishing, hallucination inducing sleep deprived miles." But it does also say this: "The Hi-Tec Badwater *& Mt. Whitney* Ultra Marathon" [Emphasis added.]

Me, running across Panamint Valley in the Badwater race in 1992
when I set the 146-mile record.

By then a complete desert devotee, I started thinking about increasingly difficult Death Valley challenges for myself. I wanted to try a solo, self-supported, unaided crossing of the 146 miles, pulling everything I would need, including water. My former crewperson, Keith Pippin, was an engineer and had crunched the numbers; he said because of the sheer volume and weight of the water I'd have to tow along, and the demands of fluid replacement in the desert, it would be impossible. So in 1995 I gave it a try. And failed. Miserably, getting only a dozen miles up the road.

But it stuck in my mind that it could be done, so I tried again in 1999. This time, I succeeded in finishing the first solo, self-supported, unaided effort across the 146 miles, which I completed in 77:46. Not unlike Al Arnold's crossing years earlier, I made my effort alone, but I didn't run in my underwear (missed opportunity?), and I had the added burden of pulling a cart that weighed 220 pounds with all my supplies, including water, food, clothing, and first aid, instead of using a support car. People drove by every six hours or so to make sure I wasn't cheating and to see that I was okay. During the midnight hours, I was completely alone. It seemed a sacred act to keep moving forward through that quiet darkness, concentrating on the task at hand while feeling inexplicably comfortable and safe in my surroundings. Later, on my way up Mount Whitney, I kept someone with me to verify that I didn't take any water from the plentiful sources there. When I said I would do this "unaided," I'd meant it, so I drank water that I had brought with me from the start.

As of this writing, I've crossed Death Valley, on this route and always in July, twenty-three times, and have gone to the summit of Mount Whitney each and every time. A couple of other old-timers have made a point of always doing the traditional route, too, especially Scott Weber, who has gone the full distance thirteen times, and Danny Westergaard, who has not only always run the traditional route (which he's done eleven times as of this writing), but also doubled back to the start for a total of 292 miles each time.

Call me stubborn, but to me, the true test always includes the mountain, starting and ending at two elevation extremes, bookending the race with difficult yet magnificent tests of conditioning. In recent years, a friend or two occasionally joined me on my hike to the summit. Of course, we secured our permits first, and I usually stopped at the portals after the desert portion, caught a ride back down to Lone Pine to sleep in a hotel, and maybe even took a day off before continuing to the top. I'm not in a hurry these days.

But it's imperative for me to go the entire distance—starting in the desert and then continuing onto the top of the mountain, I feel connected with something ineffable. Those environments speak to me, telling me or reminding me who I am. They connect me with Nature, show me how fragile life is, and how my own could change in an instant. They ground me, and I feel gratitude for being alive. And they make me feel small—so very small in the grand scheme. They bring me peace.

IN 2000, Hi-Tec bequeathed the Death Valley race to Adventure-Corps, a company founded by Chris Kostman. That year, the number of people invited to participate nearly doubled to forty-two and continued to climb every year thereafter, reaching a cap at just under one hundred. The annual Badwater 135 race has since garnered some national press, and *National Geographic* once dubbed it the toughest footrace in the world. Nowadays, fewer and fewer people who enter the race feel the need to complete the traditional 146 miles, so they don't even attempt to get a permit. Often, I don't see anyone else from the race on the mountain. For many years now, the finish has officially, unofficially, and every other kind of way been on the shoulder of Whitney, at the portals.

Since changing hands, the race is now more regulated, with stricter rules to ensure not only the runners' safety, but also that the race can continue to be held in Death Valley. (In 2014, due to a dust-up with the government, the Badwater 135 race was moved to another course altogether, but it has regained its old place since then, as well as returned to an evening start time, which it had abandoned since 1996.) This race has grown in numbers and lost some of its downhome, personal feel, but it is for the best: top ultrarunners are not only allowed to be a part of this significantly difficult race, but to be a part of the history of Death Valley and, at least, the shoulder of Mount Whitney.

The year after AdventureCorps took ownership, I went after something many people thought was truly nuts: running the traditional 146-mile course four times in a row, a Badwater Quad. This wasn't an official event; it was a challenge I devised for myself, which came about because of three key factors: ambition, a desire to make my athletic pursuits more meaningful, and my love of Death Valley.

Initially, one reason for doing the Badwater Quad was, quite simply, just to do it—another feather in my cap. I had been thinking about it for years and wanted to show that it could be done and in a fairly short period of time. No one had ever made four consecutive crossings on this route, one that had become so familiar to me that I felt a part of it. I thought, *Who better than me to attempt this? This is my proving ground.*

Then, in January 2001, a friend who knew what I was planning contacted me about using the Badwater Quad as a fund-raising event to benefit the Religious Teachers Filippini. An ultrarunner, Lisa Smith-Batchen, had been raising money for them for years, and she told me why: One of the functions of this group is to help war widows and starving children in some of the poorer countries in the world. More than just providing food, the Teachers Filippini build schools and educate women in trades that allow them to become more self-sufficient. I was completely convinced that this was a worthy cause when I learned that 100 percent of the money raised would be used to help underprivileged women and children.

As I thought about it, I could see meaningful connections: my temporary suffering would reflect the relentless suffering of the people who would be helped by it. My actions could bring attention to their difficulties, which dwarfed my own.

At the beginning on July 20, 2001, at 6:10 in the morning, the ego-based motivations dominated. I was excited to be back in my desert home, contemplating doing something no one else had even tried to accomplish before. The plan was to finish a "double" (out and back, from Badwater Basin to Mount Whitney then a reverse trip), then run in the official Badwater Ultramarathon and continue up to the summit, then go back again to the start, thus completing a second double. The reverse trips would add another five thousand feet of elevation gain, bringing the elevation gain to over twenty-four thousand feet per double for a total of 584 miles and about ninety-six thousand feet of elevation change during the Badwater Quad. It sounded like the ultimate challenge to me, and I was eager to get started.

The first crossing went well, as I took a conservative approach. For the first 146-mile stretch, I was not concerned about speed. I crossed the valley walking and running at a steady, consistent pace. Since my first outing in 1990, I had learned that, instead of the black compression shorts I'd worn eleven years ago, it was best to wear white, loosely fitting pants, which cut the pavement's radiated heat on my legs by something like twenty degrees. A kerchief or buff filled with ice was even better at keeping me cool than the "tops and tails" alone. At fifty years old and this stage of my running career, beyond my prime but in that sweet spot where determination could make up for any lack in speed, it was just a matter of putting one foot in front of the other, and we reached the top of Mount Whitney in just under forty-eight hours. This portion of the event was unremarkable, another typical crossing (if there is such a thing). It was a glorious day on the summit, and my four-person crew and I reveled in the moment, spending a short time celebrating. Lisa Smith-Batchen, Bob Haugh (a pathologist we always called "Dr. Bob"), Gary Kliewer, and Diane Grecsek were a truly all-star bunch, each of them top athletes, and all of them had gone up Mount Whitney with me. On the way down from the mountain, we laughed, joked, and for a few hours thought about nothing but enjoying the descent.

As we headed into Lone Pine, the small town just below the Whitney Portals, we began to focus on returning to Badwater Basin. The crew started planning and gathering all of the supplies—especially ice, water, and food—that would be needed for another crossing of the hot desert. My mind was on the time, as I had reached the summit in forty-eight, about twelve hours ahead of schedule. Unknown to my crew, I had visions of accelerating a bit and taking a shot at the double-crossing record set by Robert "Primus" Lambert. So, suddenly my goal shifted to returning to Badwater Basin as quickly as possible. When I told my crew members what I was planning to do, many were concerned that this new goal would jeopardize the entire Badwater Quad attempt, that I would burn out and be unable to finish. At first, some of them were angry, but they came around eventually. My charm won them over—if by "charm" I mean stubbornness.

I kept a moderate pace, and that night, I saw more scorpions than ever before. Illuminated by flashlights and the occasional crew vehicle headlights, they backed away with tails uplifted, ready to strike if we came too close. I had cut out the toe box of my shoes to accommodate the swelling of my feet, so I felt skittish imagining that one of those buggers might sting one of my toes.

The next day, nearing the motel where many of the Badwater Ultra-marathon participants and crew were staying before the race, I could see a few of the runners and Chris Kostman, the race director, coming out onto the road. Some paced me to Stovepipe Wells, running with me and giving me their support. It was a wonderful feeling to have these people beside me, acknowledging our efforts.

Hours later as night fell, it became especially challenging, as I was having to work hard to stay awake. I'd increased my pace, and my body was starting to experience the cumulative effects of the miles. My arms and neck ached, yet I was running steadily with no intent of stopping. My crew had come to the realization that I really could break the double record, and all were now supportive of that goal. Other

Badwater Ultramarathon runners started arriving during the night, and as they drove by, they offered encouragement that further motivated me. Dawn broke, and we knew that the record was in hand.

Arriving at Badwater Basin after ninety-six hours and seven minutes, we broke the old double record of 105 hours by almost nine hours and nearly managed a negative split (a faster time running back than running out). We laughed and hugged, and were twenty-three hours ahead of schedule! We danced the jig and celebrated together as a team. It was sweet victory. But looming ahead was the fact that I was entered in the actual Badwater race that would begin early the next morning, and the clock kept ticking. With our precious time ticking away, we drove back to Furnace Creek, attended the mandatory pre-race meeting, regrouped, resupplied, and got a short night's sleep. The relief crew (Courtney Boova, Ernie Rambo, and Jay Batchen, Lisa's husband) arrived. David Brooks, a freelance photographer, came on to round out the crew, and Dr. Bob, Lisa, Gary, and Diane stayed on to help. There were about four people crewing me at any given time, but now with the extra help, individual crew members could take breaks.

At 6:00 a.m. on the 25th, we started the Badwater race with the seventy-one other people entered to complete the 135-miles to the Whitney Portals. The night before had seemed short, as I was restlessly anticipating the start of the third crossing of the desert and a second journey to the top of Mount Whitney. The unpredictable weather on the mountain was worrisome, as it could stop us from reaching our goal. (Remember the hailstorm that plagued the American team back in 1987?)

Despite all that, standing at the starting line for the second time in one week, I was looking forward to getting moving again. It was great to be a part of the race, and everyone's energy made it easy to get back on the road. My muscles were slightly sore, and I had lost two or three pounds of weight over the first five days, but overall, I felt good. Headed out, I mixed walking and running, just as I had the first time. I started to think that as great as the first double experience was, the second would be no more difficult.

And it wasn't—for a while. The first twenty miles passed without incident, but soon after that I had to acknowledge the tendinitis that had begun to flare up on the front of my left shin. To combat it, we figured out how to tie a baggie of ice to the front of my leg with an Ace bandage, which served to reduce the swelling and helped me deal with the pain. Another twenty miles in, the same thing happened to my right leg. So much for uneventful. Having to contend with the ordinary task of keeping me fueled and hydrated was one thing, but now my crew was faced with wrapping my legs in ice every fifteen to thirty minutes. It became a ritual. If the ice disappeared, or if I picked up the pace even to a sustained jog, it felt like 120-volt shocks probing my legs. So they unwrapped, re-supplied ice, and rewrapped my legs over a hundred times, and we all hoped that the injury would subside during the next few days.

About sixty miles into the third crossing, I sat in the van, which was parked in an overlook area. We had decided to take a six-hour break, and I propped my legs up on a cooler with the ever-present ice bags wrapped above my ankles and my legs. I thought about the hundreds of miles I still had to go and whether I could accomplish what I had set out to do. *Am I even capable of finishing? Was my crew right? Am I flaming out?* Offers and suggestions were made for modifying the run: I could bicycle to the finish. I could literally lean on crew members; they would help in any way that they could to get the job done. Dr. Bob recommended that I quit, saying that if the swelling continued up my legs, it could cause compartment syndrome. He explained that the risks included nerve damage and a permanent foot drop, a gait abnormality that would probably kill my running career.

Trying to process this latest information, my mind drifted back to my early days running in Death Valley, to one year when I'd passed out twice; to the year when I'd doubled my ankle over on a rock and run on a second-degree sprain for the last sixty miles; to the solo crossing and the constant nosebleed that I never could control. I had finished them all but for a different reason—back then, I'd had something to prove to myself.

That's when my motivation shifted: *This Badwater Quad has very little to do with me. It is for the starving children, for my dedicated crew, for the people who set foot in this desert with great appreciation, and for everyone who demands a better, more compassionate world to live in.*

At first, Dr. Bob refused to be a part of continuing, but as I headed out onto the road, we struck a bargain. My friend, always thoughtful and caring, made me agree that if the tendinitis got any worse and moved up the leg, we'd quit. We carried on through the night, and it got no better, but also no worse. My legs became the center of my universe, and I could think of little else, but somewhere in my consciousness I held onto the idea that this suffering would mean something, would help someone who was in much worse circumstances than I was.

Late the next evening, the struggle paid off as we finished the official race at the Whitney Portals. We rested for an hour, then headed up Mount Whitney again, this time in the dark. Dr. Bob packed ice in a thermal pouch so that we could ice my legs while on the mountain. That, along with trekking poles to take some of the weight off my legs, allowed me to reach the summit in about 185 hours, setting a new triple-crossing record. We spent little time at the top, as fatigue from the exertion and sleep deprivation were obviously taking their toll. We were stumbling a bit, and I was unable to generate enough body heat to keep warm. My mind wandered, I wanted to stop moving, and I descended from the altitude in a daze.

During the next two days, I felt as if I was constantly hallucinating. My head was clouded. I could hear people talking and trying to keep my spirits up, but nothing really got through. Both nights were long and hard, and it became difficult to do anything but think about simple things like deliberately picking up my feet and letting them swing forward. Lisa spent many, many miles with me on the course through these long and difficult hours, as she had during the first double. Her dedication and nearly constant presence and support meant everything. As she gave me words of encouragement, my mind repeatedly wandered back to the day earlier when I had found—outside of myself —the strength to continue.

After we reached flat ground, it became increasingly difficult to move. Since we'd started the second double, I had slept no more than one and a half hours at a stretch. The temperatures on the desert floor had risen from the lower 110s at the start of my Badwater Quad to the mid-120s. Blisters had begun appearing on the sides and balls of my feet anywhere there was friction, making it necessary to cut off portions of my shoes, including holes in the soles. Having worn out one pair of shoes on the first double, I succeeded in wearing out a second. (I later returned the shoes to one of my sponsors, North Face, and joked, "These shoes are pretty bad, as each pair only lasted a few days.")

That last morning, the temperature was up to 126 degrees with a thirty-mile-per-hour headwind. We struggled south with Badwater Basin just seventeen miles away. I had lost about twelve pounds, and my left arm felt heavy and numb. I occasionally tucked it in my pants behind the small of my back, palm out, just so I wouldn't have to carry it anymore. This brought some relief from the chest pains that I reasoned (as well as I could) were caused by having to carry the now-useless appendage. Although my numb arm and chest pains scared me, and my legs ached with every step, on some level *it didn't matter.* I knew I was going to make it. I knew I would get to the finish with a little luck and perseverance and the continuing support of my crew. My friends Tony Di Zinno and Chris Kostman arrived to cheer me on as we neared Badwater Basin. My crew joked and was in good spirits. I regained some of my senses, and together we savored the last few miles.

The 2001 finish of my Badwater Quad.

Later, Courtney Boova wrote,

No big fanfare waited for our arrival at the finish. A few photographers were present as Marshall, along with his crew members, walked arm in arm across an ever-so-appropriate Ace bandage finish line. A douse of champagne and a few loving words from crew members while Tina Turner's "Simply the Best" played in the background were all that was needed to commemorate the finish.

I thought the finish was grand. The lack of fanfare, the solitude—it was just my crew and me and a fiery sunset reflected in a pond called Badwater. My elapsed time was approximately 253 hours: ten days and thirteen hours. Most significant, my focus had nearly completely shifted off my own ambitions and misery and onto other people. As it turned out, the event was a success in every way that mattered; ultimately, we raised over $70,000 for the Religious Teachers Filippini.

Postscript: In 2014, Lisa ran her own Badwater Quad benefiting the Teachers Filippini specifically to provide clean drinking water to villages in Ethiopia and India. She became the first woman to do it, completing the 584 miles in fourteen days, while raising hundreds of thousands of dollars to build wells.

OCCASIONALLY, someone will ask me what it takes to run in Death Valley—how do you get through the Badwater 135 race, or the traditional 146-mile course, a solo, a double, a triple, or even a quad? It takes not thinking about it too much and not bragging about your plans. It takes the support of friends who are knowledgeable or willing to learn what you'll need to complete the effort. It takes making and sticking to an agreement with yourself that you are willing to suffer and pay the price.

Of course, it also takes training. The body must be conditioned both for the miles and the heat. It doesn't come easy; it can take months and years of training, of discipline and foresight. The best training closely simulates the environment of the intended event, including weather, altitude, and ground surface. To train for heat, you may spend your summer bundled up like an Inuit; to train for cold, you may spend your winter outside when everyone else is cuddled up by the fire with a nice glass of whiskey. To get ready for long distances, you may find yourself grinding out the miles day after day, or to prepare for higher elevations, you might be running up a mountain in rarified air.

Training is not rocket science, but it requires focus and a desire to accomplish the extraordinary, regardless of whether you define "extraordinary" as something that has never been done before or something *you've* never done before. We can all do more when we don't limit our minds or think that our bodies won't adapt.

With any aspiration, we're bound to experience difficulties. Will we embrace them for their profound lessons, or shy away and forego our dreams? My advice is to go for it. Consider doing it for someone other than just yourself—raise money or awareness for a cause you believe in or dedicate your adventure to a loved one. You not only achieve or get closer to your goals, but you also gain a certain perspective that can come only from walking through the fire, which strips away the extraneous and leaves you spent, but builds your strength and stamina for the next test.

7

RETREAT

SOME PEOPLE CALL me crazy and superhuman. Maybe they think they're being complimentary, but it's backhanded at best. Doesn't it dismiss the power of human aspiration, perseverance, and strength? Dr. Murray Griffin, a friend at the University of Essex, attributes extreme endurance athletes' pursuits to a natural evolutionary impulse. Just as *Homo sapiens* has always attempted to advance intellectually and artistically, so has our species strived physically. Consider what we've accomplished in the two hundred thousand years since we first developed our lighter skeletons and big brains. Remarkable, isn't it? Even in the relatively short span of my own lifetime, I have seen people invent, break through, create, and revolutionize within dozens of fields: computing, communication, genomics, agriculture, archaeology, aviation, space exploration...the list goes on. Similarly, we modern athletes and adventurers continue to push ourselves by, for example, running across vast distances and climbing to the highest elevations.

For me, extreme sports are about following my imagination, overcoming barriers, ignoring naysayers, and defying the idea of "impossible." Whenever anyone of our species goes farther, digs deeper, or rises higher, we're obliged to re-examine limitations we've imposed on ourselves, often without ever having tested the boundaries. It's why, after years of competing in and sometimes winning organized races, I started inventing new tests of endurance, trying things that had never been done before. Originality and ingenuity plus grit have become hallmarks of my athletic career and, no matter what anyone else thinks, I consider those three to be completely sane and uniquely human traits.

Yet, when my buddy Dave Heckman revealed his plans for trekking around the perimeter of Death Valley, the largest national park in the lower forty-eight states—and the hottest place on earth—I thought he was going too far. Like many athletes, I consider this desert to be one of the toughest places on earth to test one's mettle, and I had logged thousands of miles there, both in footraces and in other feats of extreme endurance. It's earned me the nicknames "King of Badwater" and "Zen Master of Extremes," but instead of giving me confidence in his ability to succeed, my experience gave me pause. I worried about Dave walking off into the shimmering sandscape and never coming back. If he made it, this would be a truly remarkable first, but knowing what I did about the high risk of death, I thought it was more likely that I'd never see my friend again.

Should he spend weeks tromping around in extreme heat, going hundreds of miles far from any assistance and forgoing any aid, it would require burying dozens of caches of food and water plus a system for remembering where those caches were buried. If he didn't dry up in the blazing sun futilely searching for supplies, surely he'd buckle under the weight of water he'd have to carry on his back. Or else the critters would catch him. Scorpion sting? Snakebite? Bighorn sheep stampede? If he were to be injured in a remote spot with no medical help, that could be his painful end. He wouldn't be the first to perish in agony out there.

Death Valley earned its name in the mid-1800s when a gold prospector died there and the rest of his group, called '49ers, just assumed they'd wind up victims of the desert's indifference, too. Although they were rescued and survived, they had the right idea: beautiful and foreboding, Death Valley poses serious risks to those who travel in, around, and through it, and if you're foolish or simply unlucky, it can take your life. Heat-related illnesses commonly cause fatalities there; the National Park Service reported nine heat-related deaths between 1999 and 2012, and a couple of times there were three such deaths in a single year. Sometimes people vanish for a time, and their bodies are found years later. These facts, coupled with my own firsthand knowledge made this expedition sound way, way over the top.

So, when Dave asked me to join him, I told him what I was think-ing: "No. No way. Now *that's* crazy."

We discussed his idea a few times, as Dave kept finding ways to bring it up. Repeatedly, I rejected it, insisting it was much too danger-ous. He never pushed, although he wanted me to sign on, and he never took himself too seriously, either, despite fully intending to follow through. A firefighter paramedic in the San Francisco Bay area, he had served for years on the medical team at the Badwater race and competed in a 508-mile cycling race, also held in Death Valley, so he understood the peculiar ways that exertion in the desert can affect the human body. He'd personally treated people for heat-related illnesses and injuries resulting from sustained effort. He'd also camped in various parts of Death Valley and claimed it was one of his favorite things to do.

At first, his persistence made me worry for him, and then it started to amuse me. *This young pup has some serious gumption to keep badgering me about this, basically challenging me to grow a pair and wander around in the desert with him.* At thirty-eight, he was twenty-three years younger than I was, but not so young as to be foolhardy, and he began to win me over. Perhaps what recommended him most was his easygoing nature —that, and his impressive navigational skills—and although the expe-dition was still dangerous as hell and scared me plenty, it started to seem a wonderful idea. I'd told my wife, Heather, that I was done with doing anything "really extreme" a year before, but I'd recovered from the burn-out that had prompted me to make that promise. I was ready to do something fresh, new, and creative, and I became intrigued with Dave's plan. Thank goodness my wife knows me better than to believe it when I say "never again."

The challenge of the prep and planning was compelling, and the likelihood of succeeding was uncertain, both of which added to the appeal. By October of 2011, I agreed to join him.

WE BEGAN that winter to prepare for the expedition, which we eventually referred to as "Alive in Death Valley" (best to focus on success). Dave mapped out the route, a loop tracing the 425-mile perimeter of Death Valley National Park (DVNP), going over nine mountain ranges with approximately forty thousand feet in elevation gain. He scrutinized sections of a quarter-mile or shorter on Google Earth. Crucial to our survival, his work and our discussions about it took months. Our choices also made this a noteworthy endeavor: we planned to go out in July or August when both daytime and nighttime temperatures would be at their highest, and follow the boundary of DVNP as much as possible, but bury the caches outside of it, as it's illegal to dig in a National Park. We coordinated with the NPS rangers, letting them know we would be near the park to bury our caches, and they gave us information about allowable camp sites and worked with us on our film permit, which we were required to get from the Film Commission of California before photographing or filming anything. Sticking as closely to the park boundary as we could meant traversing rough mountainous terrain as well as deep, washed-out gullies and rocky desert floors. We imposed these difficulties on ourselves to ensure that our expedition wouldn't be easily replicated or written off as a walk in the park.

We decided we'd start along the eastern border, from California Highway 190 just west of Death Valley Junction, and head north, going counterclockwise up and around the park. We thought of it in chunks, each about a hundred miles (four or five days depending on difficulty):

Section 1, Heading Out. On a lopsided clock face, our starting point would be at about three o'clock, and we'd head north from there along the western border, going through the Amargosa Valley and over the Sawtooth Mountains.

Section 2, Over the Top. From one o'clock to eleven o'clock, again on a lopsided oblong, the top of the loop drifted westerly across the northern tip of Death Valley, where we'd traverse mountain ranges, a steep canyon, and three valleys (Sarcobatus Flat, the top of Death Valley, and Eureka Valley).

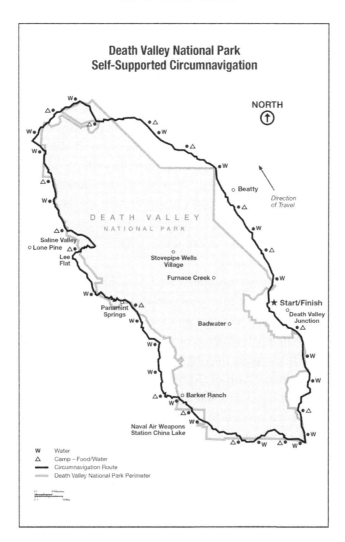

The route we took around the park in 2012.

Section 3, Down and Up and Down Again. From eleven o'clock to seven o'clock, we'd head south down the western side of the loop through Saline Valley to a major climb onto Lee Flat, then down through Panamint Valley.

Section 4, Coming Home. From seven o'clock to three o'clock, we'd go east up the canyon of Goler Wash and through the Naval Air Weapons Station at China Lake, then the final forty or more miles north under the shadow of Eagle Mountain back to the point where we'd begun. As we set the route, we calculated where we'd need water and how much, along with the type and amounts of food, as well as what other supplies we should include. We planned a system of plastic bins for storage of everything but the water, which we'd bury in prepackaged cases. We didn't always agree: Dave and I had vastly different ideas about what to eat, so we decided to pack all of it. His stash would include an assortment of endurance gels and other engineered sports "fuels" along with sardines and V8 juice. Mine would be more conventional: canned food, snacks like chips and Cheetos, soda, and packets of coffee and hot chocolate, along with some freeze-dried foods, electrolyte tablets, and ready-to-eat meals (MREs) that I'd order online from a military supply store.

More significant, we disagreed about our basic plan for the caches: Dave thought we could hike thirty miles a day and proposed that we bury the caches about that far apart and with about half the water I suggested. Although I understood his reasoning—reduce the amount of time and effort spent digging all of this into the ground—his plan spooked me. I insisted on overdoing it, burying caches closer together than we thought necessary and squirreling away a lot more water than we'd use. I felt we needed to take a "disaster preparedness" approach, given that miscalculations or unanticipated events might not be merely inconvenient; they could be deadly.

Dave acquiesced, and when we assembled our supplies to take them out to bury in the desert, we took six hundred gallons of water (to make sure we had more than enough), our food, batteries, a few pairs of socks, and toilet paper. All of it was portioned into thirty-eight plastic bins (with an extra treat tucked into a few), each with a note taped on the top of the lid offering our contact information and this plea:

Please do NOT disturb. We are making a 600-mile circumnavigation, on foot, of this area in July and Aug 2012. Our LIVES depend on our access to this food, water, and supplies. Thank you from Marshall Ulrich and Dave Heckman.

In late May of 2012, we hauled it all to Death Valley in Dave's pick-up truck and my SUV plus a trailer that I'd outfitted with ten-ply tires so that the cactus wouldn't puncture them. Dave swung the pick and I wielded the shovel about sixteen hours a day in weather that was cool by Death Valley standards, topping out at about 100 degrees each day. Each hole was around two feet deep, nearly half of them were two feet long by eighteen inches wide, and the rest were trenches about the size of a short person's grave. (We would have looked highly suspicious if there had been any passersby.) The bigger holes held our caches for overnight stays, while the smaller ones had only the water we'd need on the move. We put two caches in rock piles, because there wasn't any suitable place to dig down. As we filled each hole with the sealed containers, then dropped in the boxed six-packs of water jugs and covered them with a trash bag to keep out moisture, we sprinkled cayenne pepper in and on top of the containers then buried them with sand and dirt, hoping to deter any critters. Ultimately, we buried only 350 gallons of water and gave the remaining 250 gallons to a grateful NPS ranger, who put them in storage at a station in Cow Creek for future use.

To be self-supported, we buried thirty-five caches of water, food, and supplies.

It took us six days to get everything into the ground and documented for retrieval, noting GPS coordinates and taking photographs of anything that might serve as a landmark. Neither of us are clock-watchers, though, and we were in sync while we were working, especially about getting it done no matter how long it took. This boded well for the expedition itself: clearly we'd make a good team. We also discovered that we had compatible senses of humor, and I started thinking Dave's dry wit would come in handy in the desert. After finishing our big dig and returning to Dave's home in Northern California, we took his two sons, Dylan (a few months old) and Jack (three years), on a long walk around Half Moon Bay, and I loved watching him interact with his little guys. So positive and encouraging, never a cross word, and it was obvious Jack picked up on all that and helped to entertain Dylan, making him laugh as they walked with the youngest in the stroller for well over an hour. All of this confirmed my decision to undertake this expedition with Dave.

As we talked about it, he expressed his own reason for taking on this kind of outdoor adventure: paradoxically, by getting outside and exposing yourself to the elements, he explained, "You're going inside yourself...to discover things you can't discover unless you do something like this."

Like me, he was also drawn to the chance to experience the beauty of the desert in a new way, and to throw off the trappings of our daily lives, which we both referred to as "all the crap we don't need." Although we had somewhat over-packed our caches, we were committed to keeping the loads we'd have to carry light. It would include only the essentials, and it would all have to fit in our Deuter Spectro (sponsor-provided) backpacks. Depending on the amount of water we needed at any time, we'd each carry twenty-five to fifty-five pounds on our backs, and the following:

- Three 100 oz. bladders for water, which we'd fill according to expected demand, based on air temperatures and the roughness of terrain
- Leki carbonite trekking poles (sponsor-provided)
- Sleeping pad
- Bivvy sack
- Light sleeping bag

- Buffs for dust protection and water cooling
- Multitool or knife
- Emergency blanket (space blanket)
- Light cord and a couple of bungees
- Hat or scarf
- Sunglasses
- Headlamp
- Sanitary wipes and toilet paper
- Toothbrush
- Engo blister prevention patches (sponsor-provided)
- Sportslick (sponsor-provided)
- Dermatone sunscreen and lip protection (sponsor-provided)

Only in Dave's pack:

- Long-sleeved fleece pullover
- GPS unit
- Still camera with the cache photos and our map
- Satellite phone

Only in my pack:

- Lightweight down sweater
- Small stove
- Titanium cooking pot and coffee cup
- Tracking device
- 3D HD video camera
- Titanium trowel

We were outfitted with clothes and boots by sponsors: a T-shirt, pants, and underwear from ExOfficio; socks from Balega; and hikers from Hoka One One. We didn't pack a change of clothes, so that was all we wore, except for our wedding rings and watches, and we stuffed the watches into our packs soon after departure.

THAT JULY, Dave and I returned to Death Valley for the annual Badwater race, where I competed and he served as medic, just as we both had done so many times before; he and I both viewed the race as preparation for the main event, the DVNP circumnavigation expedition—circumnav for short. To round out his training, four or five times prior to the race, Dave had gone hiking for a few hours with a heavy backpack. Being fit already and accustomed to combatting heat stress in his job as a firefighter, he considered that sufficient.

My plan was more aggressive. At sixty-one years old, I was more cautious and more experienced. So, in addition to my year-round conditioning—running about twenty miles per week in the fall, picking it up to forty miles per week during the late winter, and gradually increasing to a peak distance of about eighty miles per week in the final two months before Badwater—I had put myself through an intensive heat-training regimen. I'd spent the six weeks prior to arriving in Death Valley hitting the sauna three or four times a week, sweating it out for an hour to an hour and a half in temperatures of 160 to 180 degrees Fahrenheit. I'd learned the importance of this heat acclimation from the Badwater old-timers, and had used this routine to get ready to run in desert conditions for many years. One of the key lessons I learned from competing in Death Valley is that nothing assures suffering to the point of DNF ("did not finish") like underestimating the impact of those desert temperatures—and the human body does have a remarkable ability to adapt, to become more efficient in the absorption of water and to regulate temperature, if you put in the time to prepare.

Between July 11 and 12, just a few days before the start gun went off for the 2012 race, Death Valley sizzled. The high temperature on that Wednesday hit 128 degrees F, and the low temperature on Thursday morning dropped to only 107 degrees F, giving those twenty-four hours the warmest average temperature on record, a scorching 117.5 degrees F.[1] Starting on Monday, the race itself was relatively uneventful for me, as I had decided not to push too hard but instead to treat it like a 135-mile training run. At one point, I stopped at a hotel to nap for several hours, which of course no one does if they are trying for a personal best. I finished in forty-one hours and fifty-five minutes, not a particularly fast time for me, but I defended my record of finishing more Badwater Ultramarathon races than anyone else as I crossed the finish line for the eighteenth time. After a day's rest with some pizza and beer, I set my sights on the DVNP expedition. Over the next few days, Dave and I checked on a couple of caches to make sure they were all right, assuming that if they were good, the others would be also. We also walked off-road for about eighteen miles from the Badwater basin toward Furnace Creek to explore the salt-pan terrain and fine-tune our equipment and clothing. After that, we put our feet up and considered our imminent ordeal.

We wouldn't be entirely alone, however. Heather and a friend, Roger Kaufhold, had stayed with us after all the Badwater racers, staff, and crew left the area, planning to be our "sweep" once we were underway. The two of them would stop at designated points to collect and remove our trash, and give us only encouragement if they happened to see us—we didn't plan rendezvous points, but we might get lucky. If we had forgotten to pack an item, or decided after the fact that we needed something, they wouldn't provide it. Hell, yeah, it would be nice to have a cold drink or hang out under an umbrella, but we were intent on making this difficult, remember? We'd complete the trip completely self-supported, so their job was strictly to monitor our progress and help us leave no trace.

On July 22, we were up early and drove to our starting point near Bat Mountain. I felt anxious, aware that we would encounter many unanticipated obstacles. Outwardly relaxed, I wasn't confident we could pull it off. As Heather drove, I looked out the window, watching mesquite bushes whizz by, and the colors of the sunrise sweep over the desert floor. The four of us could see the pass Dave and I would have to navigate below, a few miles off in the distance, and I thought about how lucky I was to have Heather by my side, supporting me as she had so many times before. I thought about each of my children and how blessed I was to be their father.

At about 6:00 a.m., Dave and I said goodbye to Heather and Roger, then struck out heading north. We started at a brisk walking pace, about three and a half miles per hour, and headed up a long grade toward the pass below Bat Mountain, talking almost incessantly about

the terrain, what we might face, and our relief at finally being underway. We laughed and joked, lifting some of the weight of seriousness
off our shoulders. Recovering that first water cache at mile twelve was
exciting. Approaching with apprehension that we wouldn't be able to
do it, we nonetheless found the spot with the aid of our GPS, and we
also remembered it by sight even though there was no indication that
anything had been buried there—another encouraging sign.

The jugs were intact! We dug quickly and pulled out the water,
chanting, "All right! All right!" In celebration, I choked down an energy
bar I retrieved from my backpack and chased it with copious amounts
of water, then Dave and I filled our water bladders and doused
ourselves with the rest. Assured that we'd be able to find more of our
caches and that there would be water and supplies in them, we
continued on to where we'd stop for the night, around mile twenty-
five. During the second half of the day, we were much quieter, and the
trekking seemed endless. Dave lagged behind at times, hanging his
head, sometimes wandering and weaving instead of walking a straight
line. He stopped and fidgeted more than seemed normal for him, and
though he didn't say a word about what was going on, it became
obvious that he was suffering in the heat.

Even with our first success, we worried as we approached our stopping point for the day. Would the cache hold another intact resupply
of water? Would our food still be edible? Would we actually find the
damn thing? Sure enough, we did, and everything was in order,
including a few sundries for comfort: toilet paper, a soda (such a treat!),
and fuel tablets for the little stove I'd insisted on carrying. Dave
downed some V8 and a can of beef stew, content to eat it without
heating it first. Although it was a hot day (Death Valley was still
topping the U.S. temperature charts and had been for a while, hitting
121 degrees F on our first day[2]), I fired up the stove and had my first
taste of reconstituted freeze-dried food for this trip: beef stroganoff.
Not bad!

After dinner, we prepared to wash up and bed down, but then...
Wait a minute. Who forgot the soap? After futilely checking and double-
checking our stash, we gave up. Oh, well, we'd make do without it.
How bad could it get, anyway? (Pretty bad, as it turned out.) We rinsed

out our things and poured water over ourselves to get "clean," then wandered around naked for about ten minutes while our clothes dried quickly in the sun.

No doubt we were both thinking much the same thing. That first day had shown us what we were in for: wind, heat, scarce shade, sand, rock, and sparse desert vegetation underfoot, along with the necessity of avoiding old mine shafts, as we made our way in as straight a line as possible. Conversation had all but stopped while we instead relaxed into the solitude and quiet companionship as we moved on without any outside distractions. Despite the discomforts of the day, here we were finally able to think and breathe without the sidetracking and suffocating pressures of everyday life.

After all that, rest was intensely satisfying. Dave and I got into our sleeping bags when the sun went down, around 8:00 p.m. I covered myself with a netted bivvy to ward off any nighttime creatures. With a "mattress" of the desert floor and a thin pad, I settled in quickly then slept soundly, waking up surprisingly relaxed and recharged when it was still quite dark and nearly silent, perhaps 4:00 a.m. Dave was about thirty feet away, and as far as I knew hadn't made a sound all night. In fact, he was completely silent until he started having a muted conversation with himself just after waking. During the rest of the trip, he regularly gave himself pep talks like this before rising and again at night before sleeping, a reassuring sound for both of us each morning and evening.

That morning, we started a routine that would last the duration of our trip: getting up with the first light and going three or four miles before the sun was up, then slowing down to compensate for the increased effort and the need to take in more fluids as the temperature climbed. We continued until the sun dipped down, then stopped, made camp for the night, and ate something substantial, consuming about 80 percent of our calories in the relative cool of the evening. It proved unbearable to stop during the middle of the day unless we could shelter under a mesquite bush for a few minutes, as the slight breeze created by walking was preferable to the stultifying heat of standing still.

During our second day, Dave was beset with nausea and diarrhea, having to stop about twice an hour to relieve himself. (That same day, I picked up a 1978 penny in the dirt along the side of an old miner's road. I wondered whether it would be lucky or not, given Dave's situation.) We thought his heat exhaustion was worsening, but by the third day, we figured out that the V8 was to blame: the highly fibrous canned vegetable juice was going straight through him, and as soon as he stopped drinking the stuff, his diarrhea stopped, too. By then, though, Dave was dehydrated, tired, and weak. He told me later that he had felt so incredibly sick that if there had been a ride out, he would have taken it.

By day four, Dave had recovered for the most part, and we had reached Last Chance Canyon, where we planned to climb to the northernmost tip of DVNP. Not only had his stomach settled down, but we were also in a rhythm, having established a routine with one day much like the next. The terrain varied wildly, however. During the nearly vertical ascent out of Last Chance Canyon, we were using our climbing skills to get up and out, scaling rocks and balancing the weight of our packs carefully to make sure we didn't fall backward off the fifty-foot drop down to the bottom. When we weren't attacking a crumbled dirt and rock face like this or climbing up and over a mountain, the flats were valleys, gullies, and foothills covered in sand, sometimes mixed with dirt or fine gravel. For a few hours, we might be surrounded by cliff-like dirt walls with Pinyon-juniper trees growing from the floor or hanging precariously onto the sides, and then later descend to lower elevations with creosote bushes and desert holly growing among the occasional cactus and yucca plants.

During water stops and at the end of each day, we were exhilarated all over again to uncover a cache, make our meals (soon enough, Dave gave up his engineered foods, opting instead to share my "real food"), wash ourselves (we did miss the soap, never feeling as if we were truly clean, always wearing clothes that felt stiff and smelled stinky), talk for a few minutes, then lie down with only the stars overhead. After a couple of nights, I abandoned the bivvy as I had become one with the elements.

We simply moved all day, ate, and then slept. We had watches, but never consulted them, and somehow we were in tune with each other and our surroundings. Occasionally, we talked, but only if we had something funny or important to say, which was more likely to happen when we were moving. Dave ranted about flat-billed ball caps and the people who wear them, which made me laugh and distracted us from discomforts, and I grumbled about lame politicians. We'd joke about how "cool" it was in the desert. Dave twisted a mini bungee strap into a snakelike plaything and would scold "Tiny Bungee" whenever it went missing, then shower it with kisses whenever it resurfaced. It was absurd and hilarious. Quite earnestly, we also lamented that everyone else was missing out on all the fun and the pristine environment.

After the first week, we started waking up in the middle of the night, still not saying much but eating a few bites of food and taking care of any necessities, then nodding off again until just before first light. At the time, I attributed it to sleeping in relatively hot overnight lows, which were mostly in the mid-80s to 90°F or above.[3] After a day in the sun, with highs nearing 120°F every day, this felt surprisingly cool, but I assumed we were not fully acclimated to the heat. Later, I found out how wrong I was. We were actually acclimating to our new environment exceptionally well and experiencing "split sleep," which is an ancient and nearly forgotten pattern we humans quit after the electric lightbulb was invented. The book *Dreamland* provides some insight on this, as it presents a history professor's findings about life before the introduction of artificial light sources:

> The time between the two bouts of sleep was a natural and expected part of the night and, depending on your needs, was spent praying, reading, contemplating your dreams, urinating, or having sex.[4]

The professor stopped short of concluding that the way we sleep now is unnatural, but in the meanwhile, a psychiatrist was conducting a research experiment in which he deprived subjects of artificial light so that he could mimic the rhythms of early human life. Eventually, they all started this segmented sleep, too, just like Dave and me, waking up a little after midnight, hanging out for a while, then dropping off again until morning. Based on this and other studies, the solid night's sleep that's the quest of every insomniac is a departure from our natural sleep pattern. We have adapted, or most of us have, which makes me wonder: What number of people diagnosed with sleep disorders just have a stronger internal clock, unpersuaded by modern life? Indulge my digression, here. I hope it provides insight into one of those mysterious things we rediscover when we let go of some of our conveniences. Something to think about when you're lying there in the middle of the night, perhaps.

Split sleep was an interesting discovery for us, made possible by Death Valley's natural darkness. There, the vast black of the night sky, lit only by pinpoints of brilliance from billions of stars, remains almost entirely unpolluted by artificial light. This is such a rare and remarkable thing to experience that an organization called the International Dark-Sky Association (IDA) works not only to preserve places like this, but also to identify the effects of light pollution on human health, wildlife, and climate change and advocate for abolishing unnecessary or particularly harmful types of artificial light. We had little use for flashlights, as the constellations were enough, and when the moon was bright, we could see for miles into the distance.

This trip was largely about doing without: electric lights, refrigeration, air conditioning, soap. You might consider their absence an inconvenience, but in many ways it was just the opposite. One of the perks of spending extended time in Death Valley was the serenity that came from turning all the gadgets off, from removing the distractions of ringing and dinging and pinging, as Richard Louv puts it in *The Nature Principle*. Like *Dreamland*, this book scientifically validates what I've personally experienced: the best antidote for stress, fatigue, feelings of alienation (spiritual disconnection and separation from your surroundings), complacency (both physical and emotional), and plain old boredom is simply getting outdoors. Declaring that "nature is the ultimate antidepressant," Louv echoes my own sentiments: the more high-tech we become, the more nature we need. He asserts, "... a reconnection to the natural world is fundamental to human health, well-being, spirit, and survival."

All this to say that we unwound and found ourselves feeling more grounded once we were far away from the commotion of civilization and instead paid nearly singular attention to the terrain and the landscape, to the feel of the air around us and the weight and balance of

the few belongings we carried. I hadn't brought a single extra amuse-
ment, not so much as a crossword puzzle, and I relished the opportunity to shut off the chatter and clatter. With the exception of my wife
and family, and perhaps my bed, I can't say I missed any of it.

In fact, as we neared the end of our first week, we began to feel so
comfortable that we were almost cocky, nearly complacent. We had
grown accustomed to the weather, and temperatures that would seem
scorching to most people felt commonplace to us. We had absolutely
no encounters with wildlife and had stopped worrying about that altogether. We saw birds anywhere there was water (perhaps every thirty
or forty miles), as the crows and ravens showed up reliably for any
small oasis. Occasionally at night, we heard coyotes howling in the
distance and found it comforting; their yipping and yowling, though it
might have sounded like distress calls or threats to an outsider, gave us
a sense of safety and unity with our surroundings. The "song dogs"
were communicating with one another, after all, strengthening social
bonds.

Dave and I indulged the illusion that we were becoming one with
the desert—it is a delightful thought—but we were also aware that, in
truth, we were no more "living off the land" than an urban apartment-
dweller who can go to the corner market. We had planned and
prepared all provisions, and that, too, was a comfort—a luxury, really.
Every time we recovered a cache, we felt as if we'd just rolled up to the
Ritz.

However, not everything went smoothly. We lost one cache, never
finding our burial spot; in another, we'd packed the water upside down
and found the jugs were all dry, along with a bunch of dead insects that
had been drawn to the leak but decimated by the cayenne. These were
minor issues, as we had supplied ourselves with more food and water
than we needed and we regularly carried more water than we'd drink.
One day, though, we had a close call that left me thinking that all my
fear and worry about this trip had been well-founded.

On day eight, we went into Saline Valley in the third section of the
expedition, "Down and Up and Down Again." We were faced with two
not-great choices for getting out of the valley, either 1) taking a route
that would cut off a portion of the boundary of the park, which we

were trying to follow as closely as possible, or 2) going down about halfway through the length of Saline Valley then popping out above it, which would require us to climb about six thousand feet over two miles and to hike another ten miles or so before we'd arrive at Lee Flat. We chose the latter.

About two hours into the ascent, making our way over loose sand, dirt, and small rocks, we realized we would run out of water well before we reached the top, and then we still had a ways to go after that. We had carried about a gallon and a half between us, which we discovered too late was only about half of what we needed. Trying to conserve water the second half of the way up, I became dehydrated and started drifting in and out of consciousness while climbing, and I was struggling and straggling behind. Dave kept us moving, as I had begun stopping in any sliver of shade, seeking out the cover of mesquite bushes and Joshua trees, then slipping into a sleep-like state, yielding to the tug of giving up, feeling how much easier it would be to do that than to fight. My blood pressure had gotten so low that I was drifting off every fifteen to thirty minutes. Ahead of me in the distance, Dave yelled to snap me out of it. About the third time he roused me, he realized that my condition was dire, and that we'd both be goners if we kept moving at my pace. He came back to me and took on the extra load of my backpack then urged me to my feet, knowing that my heart was having trouble pumping the thick blood to my brain, and if he let me nap, I'd never wake up.

Without help from Dave Heckman, this could have been the last image of me...taken high above Saline Valley.

Relieved of that extra twenty or so pounds, I started to move on more reliably, and Dave muscled us through the next couple of miles to the crest. We had only the most meager amount of water remaining, only enough to take a tiny sip, swish it around and wet the tongue, swallow, and immediately feel thirsty and dry again. And then it was completely gone. My mental state improved slightly once we were headed downhill—I wasn't staggering or stopping anymore—but we still had miles to go. Meanwhile, I later found out, Heather and Roger were watching our tracker and were worrying, as our slow movement had signaled our distress, but there was no way they could get to us. We were entirely on our own.

When we finally reached the cache, Dave and I sat down and looked at each other. There were no words, but our eyes communicated clearly: *We dodged a huge f-ing bullet.* All thanks to Dave.

Hunched over the sand, we dug methodically, then each pulled a gallon jug and guzzled. That feeling...indescribable except for intense gratitude...like "Thank you, Jesus," times two thousand. We had six gallons in this overnight cache and easily polished off one each in the first hour. We sipped all through the evening and the dark hours and, remarkably, recovered reasonably quickly. I imagined the cells in my body as molecular sponges, reconstituting as the water hit them, soaking it all up. Dave and I were uncharacteristically chatty that night, joshing with each other and yucking it up after our scrape.

Just before the next sunrise, we woke up (Dave's pep talk that morning included some words of thanks about having survived the previous day's ordeal) and set off, wary but determined. Within a couple of hours, we reached a Joshua tree forest with hundreds if not thousands of these giants set far apart. Each stood at a height at least three times my own, eighteen-foot trunks forking up into about a dozen branches, each topped with green spikes. They looked like something out of a book by Dr. Seuss; the effect was magical, otherworldly, healing.

Though the trees provided ample shade, we were at about five thousand feet, so the air felt cool and we didn't need to indulge; instead, we admired the play of light and walked through it like children who'd wandered into an enchanted forest. Being in that place allowed us to reconnect with a sense of safety in nature. All cockiness was gone. We had regained a proper respect and with it our wonder at the beauty all around us. Over the next two days, we continued south and hit the highway, then turned east and dropped down after a few miles to pass the Panamint Springs Resort, where sightseers in Death Valley can camp, park their RVs, gas up, shop at the general store, get a drink at the bar, and grab a bite in the restaurant—none of which we did. We stopped and sat down on the ground, leaning against a stone wall in the shade to refresh ourselves, lingering there and chatting with Heather and Roger for an hour or more before we headed back out to the middle of Panamint Valley.

That night, ten days into our expedition, a storm crackled and poured, delivering huge amounts of rain around us and farther down, where it created a six-inch pool of water that stretched a mile one direction and two miles in the other. Just as the first drops started to fall, Dave and I decided to seek higher ground so that we wouldn't be standing in water when lightning struck. Yet even after we moved up a hill, it became clear that we'd still be in the downpour, and we had to strategize. *Should we allow ourselves to get drenched and risk hypothermia?* Given how conditioned we'd become to high temperatures, even a mild chill could bring on shivering, weakness, confusion, discoordination, and, possibly, death. *Or should we shelter under an emergency blanket to stay dry and warm?* The problem there, though, was that our space blanket was covered in microthin aluminum, so it would become a huge lightning rod. *The hell with it,* we agreed, *we pick lightning rod over hypothermia.* We huddled together for at least an hour, talking mostly about how scared we were and how, if our hair started standing on end, we'd toss the blanket and run in opposite directions. We were lucky, though, and despite electricity popping all around us, we emerged dry and unhurt once it was over.

The next day, we continued south across Panamint Valley, then toward the old, almost-abandoned village of Ballarat, where mass murderer Charles Manson's pickup truck continues to weather in the harsh sun and a sign on one of the buildings notes that it's the last chance for "Naked Burro Dancing." We walked parallel to the shallow lake the rainstorm had created, as well as some swampy areas that were homes to several burros (they were all naked as far as I could tell) and a few mining trucks passed us on Indian Ranch Road. Some of the drivers had flat-billed hats, which sent Dave off on another hilarious tirade about them. We spent a hot, humid night near the lake.

Around noon the following day, at the bottom of Goler Wash, we recovered a cache of water then marched on into the wash, where we'd stashed just a bit more water in a pile of rocks. This would have to last until late the next day, so we stocked up. There hadn't been anywhere to put a cache between this place and thirty miles away, where we'd exit China Lakes and enter Death Valley once again. We'd be almost completely off-road and our route would stay inside the national park's borders then in the China Lakes bombing area, where burying anything was forbidden and foolish. So I put 2.5 gallons on my back and carried two gallons in each hand, and Dave took just a half-gallon or so less than that, shoving a full jug into his pack. Still gun-shy from our nearly fatal climb out of the Saline Valley, we were willing to carry extra weight if it meant we'd avoid running out of water. That wasn't a risk we'd take again, and we were sure this section was the most risky because of our lack of access to...well, anything.

A gallon lighter and about four miles from the rock pile, we spotted Barker Ranch, where Manson and his "family" had hidden from police in 1969. Now deserted but still creepy, the 1930s homestead stands like a macabre museum with the burned-out house's foundation and parts of the structure still standing, including the small bathroom where Manson crouched under the sink before being apprehended. Inside an outbuilding, we read handwritten messages, some commemorating the criminal ("May he live forever") and some condemning him ("He'll rot in hell!")

We'd planned to camp overnight there, so we took our time exploring. The place was disturbing; my skin crawled at the thought of the mass murders his group had committed. And although Dave decided to sleep on the front porch, I didn't have the stomach for it and set up my gear down in a wash about a hundred feet away.

After dark, we were both surprised to hear a vehicle coming up the ranch road, as it's isolated and remote, virtually unmarked except for a couple of fence posts and tangled barbed wire. The familiar SUV came closer, and Dave and I were all smiles, knowing that we'd get a brief visit with Heather and Roger. They'd brought another friend, Rick Barraff, who'd go with us for a while and document this part of the expedition with photos. That evening, all five of us spent the night there after exploring the grounds and exclaiming over the writing on the walls. Having Heather, Roger, and Rick with us would have made for a perfect night, except for the grisly history of the ranch. Heck, the National Park Service won't allow sniffer dogs on the property, as some theorize there may be victims buried up there. We talked about Manson and his cult followers, marveling at how he had manipulated so many people to carry out his gruesome mission.

The next morning when Dave, Rick, and I got up in the dark, I was more than ready to move on. We passed another ranch with a skull-and-crossbones warning, KEEP OUT. We trod softly across the private property, unsure if it was occupied, and certain that if it was, anyone inside would be packing. We got through there without incident, and, as we entered the China Lakes bombing area, we saw four-foot dud missiles scatter-planted in the sand, those that had been shot off, plunged into the ground nose first, and never exploded. Leery of them (maybe they could still be detonated?), I stopped to snap photos anyway. When we eventually got to a road, we passed through a wire gate and turned around to read the sign warning people away from the place: DANGER! EXPLOSIVE ORDNANCE OPERATIONS—KEEP OUT!

Meanwhile, Rick, who is a fine athlete but hadn't trained for the heat, was suffering. Although Dave and I had almost forgotten that the temperatures were unusually hot, Rick felt as if he'd been thrown into the fire. He did stick it out for another day, and then he told us he'd had enough. Heather and Roger picked him up on day fourteen along Owl Hole Springs Road on the southern border of the park. Waving goodbye, he wished us luck and mentioned something about enjoying a cold beer later. That's what he said, but I'm sure what he meant was "So long, suckers."

By then, we knew we had only a few more days ahead of us, just another twenty miles or so heading east and then forty or fifty miles travelling north. We were more than three hundred miles and a couple of weeks into this adventure, and we had gained some confidence that we'd finish. Just to remind us that it wouldn't be easy, however, the last evening we spent in the southern part of Death Valley, the low for the night of 107°F was the same as the high for the next day anywhere else in the United States. Even though we were acclimated, that night felt disgustingly hot. We slept through some of the record-setting heat, although it kept us awake through a good portion of the night.

When we headed north on the border of Death Valley we looked for our next cache, but couldn't find it. We'd buried it along the side of the road in a berm of rocks and sand, and when we arrived at the place, it had all been rearranged, probably during some roadwork. Fortunately, we had enough water with us that we knew we'd be all right. Of course we were lucky: Dave found his own lucky penny around that time, a 1906 Indian head.

Not long after that, an NPS ranger approached us, chiding us for leaving litter in the park. He'd picked up some empty water jugs and a box before Heather and Roger had arrived to retrieve them, and he was pissed. He also tried to tell us that there was certainly enough water in the valley that someone (himself, in particular) could easily do this circumnavigation without burying caches. We raised our eyebrows but didn't argue, and he let us continue on. Dave and I talked about the guy for miles, what a dick he was compared to all of the other park rangers we had met in the valley over the years. We found out later that he'd also met Heather and Roger, and he'd accused them of driving off-road near Owl Hole Springs Road, a definite no-no. They hadn't, and told the ranger as much, but he took a picture of the SUV's tires to compare the tread, anyway. We never heard from him again, thankfully. Besides, what would he have charged us with? Obeying all the rules?

As we walked toward our finish line the next morning, right where we had started near the foot of Bat Mountain, we could see Heather and Roger waiting for us. They had come out to take pictures, and we could see them in front of the SUV from afar. Completing our journey at 9:49 a.m., we were greeted with congratulations and jubilation, and Dave and I quietly thanked them. All of us hugged and laughed, but the mood was subdued. Dave and I were proud of ourselves, but more than anything else, we were simply amazed that we had gotten through it. I felt at peace with the effort we'd made, something like I've experienced on mountain summits. Though the environments could not be more different at the top of Everest or in Death Valley, the two extremes had offered up much the same result: a feeling of wonder that I'd had the opportunity to test myself in this place, and gratitude for my luck in making it out alive, especially given our serious miscalculation climbing out of Saline Valley.

At the car, Heather handed Dave an ice cube from the cooler. When his mouth encountered it, the rest of us stared at him then started laughing. His reaction was nearly pornographic, that frozen bit of water completely rocking his world. He wasn't trying to be funny, but we found it hilarious and couldn't stop giggling. After we regained our composure, the four of us got in the SUV to drive about twenty-five miles to Furnace Creek, where we could get a snack and take care of some business before heading on to Lone Pine to rest. After Dave and I sat down in the car seats (what a strange feeling—cushioning! back support!), Heather turned on the engine, and then the air conditioner blew, feeling super-charged and freezing. Another shock to the system—we had to turn it down or start shivering. Then the tires crunched over the rocks and we were underway, travelling at something like forty miles per hour, and I clenched the dash in fear. It was as if I had *never* gone so fast before; Dave and I were both afraid, completely out of our element. Heather slowed down and we made our way to Furnace Creek.

Once we arrived, we had pizza, ice cream, and beer. You'd think we were at a five-star restaurant, gauging by our reaction to the food. Gauging by our appearance and hygiene, however, not so much. Dave and I both had scruffy beards, and our clothes were hanging off our bodies, as Dave had lost twenty-five pounds, and I had lost ten.

Also, we stank. If we hadn't forgotten the soap, I'm sure we wouldn't have been so pungent, as the odor was not emanating from our bodies. The heat of the desert had been cleansing as it flushed out the pores, but our clothes were holding the effects of sixteen days' worth of dirt and no suds.

*The desert ruled our bodies, as evidenced by these before and after
photos, knowing that a leaner physique cools more efficiently.*

After eating, Dave and I toweled off and changed clothes, then
Heather, Dave, and I said goodbye to Roger, who headed back to
Colorado towing the supply trailer home for us. Dave climbed into his
pickup truck, Heather and I got into the SUV, and the three of us
went to Lone Pine, a couple of hours' drive away.

We checked in at The Trails, a modest motel with pretty basic
amenities, but of course it felt outrageously luxurious. We showered!
We swam in the pool! We sat in chairs with backs! We went to the
bathroom in a toilet! I stretched out on the king-sized bed next to my
wife and thought that this was the best feeling in the world. To be
clear, though, it was Heather and not the bed that made me so happy. I
had become accustomed to my sleeping pad and found it comfortable
enough. On the other hand, traffic noise seemed louder and more irri-
tating than I remembered, interfering with my peace of mind. When
we turned on the TV that night, it was truly strange to see the bright
pictures piercing through the dark of our room. Re-entering the
modern world required more than a few adjustments.

We spent the next day with our dear friends Ben and Denise Jones,
whom we've known for years. Ben kept records of crossings from
Badwater to the summit of Mount Whitney for more than fifteen
years, documenting all crossings from 1977 until he passed along the
record-keeping in 2006. He still loves to photograph athletes in Death

Valley, and he has been present at the start or finish of all my individual exploits there. He's also a physician and has the unpleasant task of performing an autopsy whenever someone dies in the valley.

Denise has become the go-to person for help with any foot problems that develop during the race; she is sometimes referred to as The Blister Queen. Everyone who runs the Badwater Ultramarathon considers the two of them the honorary mayor and first lady of Badwater. They're also just good people, and we were delighted that they'd once again taken time to visit with us.

We went to Ben and Denise's home around mid-morning and spent a few hours talking about our adventure and catching up. We went out for pizza, where my friend Chris Frost joined us. Later on, Chris and I went to arrange our gear for one of my favorite mountain hikes, while Denise took Heather to her salon and pampered her with a new cut and color. The next day, Chris and I made the twenty-two-mile hike up and down Mount Whitney, to me a fitting end to this grueling but incredibly gratifying adventure. As always, it was cold at the top—I had to wear a fleece jacket, hat, and gloves to keep warm in the near-freezing weather (such a contrast!)—and Chris suffered from altitude sickness, but throughout the hike and once we were safely down again, I was in a state of intense gratitude for so many opportunities to explore all kinds of environments, especially the stretch between Badwater Basin and Mount Whitney.

Talking to Dave on the phone after we had both returned to our homes, we shared a genuine nostalgia for our trip. Both of us wanted to go back into the desert, feeling a primal urge to shed the comforts, conveniences, and "crap" that we had nearly immediately reassimilated into our lives. Together, we had trekked through valleys, up canyons, over mountains, across sand flats, down washes, among Joshua trees, past sand dunes and dried salt lakes, through pinyon pine and juniper forests, up and down hills, past marshes created by underground springs, along old railroad beds, and on some roads. We'd also seen some oddball monuments built by folks who may have baked their brains in the desert sun (or otherwise) a bit too much. We'd found old ruins of rock foundations, a salt tram used to move sodium chloride and a few daredevil humans over a mountain, cabins, and smelters and been surprised to come across wells, car parts, winches, bathing pools, towers, and mine shafts. If we allowed ourselves a moment of metaphysical reflection, we could say that we'd travelled with ghosts of the Timbisha Shoshone and old miners, prospectors, and explorers.

Most significantly, we had experienced deep quiet of the mind and soul. The desert was regenerative, soothing. As Dave and I surrendered ourselves to the forces of nature, our inner selves were profoundly shifted. It had provided us with tranquility that washed over us again and again. Looking back, we could re-experience it, feel that cleansing peace by drawing on memories of a simplicity that comes only from being immersed in nature. Despite cruel conditions and occasional threats, we had felt both challenged and rewarded by the environment and what it had to offer us if we just looked and listened. The lack of distractions was most remarkable. It was calming to immerse ourselves in the dark and stillness of night and the silence and solitude of day.

Not long after our return from Death Valley, someone asked Dave, "What nightmare were you having to come up with this adventure?" Dave shook his head. Aside from getting married and having kids, he said, "It ended up being the best idea I've ever had."

UNKNOWN TO US, around the time we arrived in Furnace Creek to rest, Michael Konda (Popov) set off on a six-mile run across Badwater Basin in Death Valley. A fellow endurance athlete I'd known for about a year, he was one of the most friendly, energetic ultrarunners I've ever met. If I'd had a chance to see him that day, I might have clapped him on his broad back and offered some advice. He was a remarkable runner who always planned carefully and trained hard for every effort, and he knew a bit about Death Valley, as he'd crewed at the Badwater Ultramarathon. But it is an unforgiving environment unlike any other, and given Michael's linebacker's body (heavier than most runners), I would have questioned the wisdom of taking off across the salt bogs. Frankly, I would have questioned anyone considering it, and I would never do it myself. In 1991, Patrick Hodges had attempted nearly the

same route as a birthday present for himself and died of exposure less
than a mile from his vehicle on the return trip across the basin. I
might have insisted that Michael carry more water (after what Dave
and I went through, I'm now extremely cautious about water even in
less severe conditions), and I probably would have tried to dissuade
him altogether. But I didn't see him that day, and besides, ultrarunners
are a notoriously stubborn lot, thinking they can survive anything.

The mercury was hanging at about 120°F that afternoon and,
completely out of character, he made the decision to run across the
basin on the spur of the moment as he and his partner, Sarah Spelt,
were exploring Death Valley for a future race he might organize. His
intention was to head over the salt flat from West Side Road to
Badwater Road, where Sarah would pick him up. They stopped the car
at a spot called Shorty's Grave, where they could easily see an outcrop-
ping of black rock at his intended finish line, which he thought was the
parking lot where the Badwater Ultramarathon started each year. He
grabbed his backpack with tracker and cellphone, along with seventy-
two ounces of water, hugged and reassured Sarah—"Don't start your
worry watch for three hours," he told her—and then set out.[5]

He might have been okay if he'd actually made it to their
rendezvous point. However, he'd wound up about two miles south of
the parking area. Overheated and exhausted, he then got into a car
with some tourists who drove him four miles even farther south by
mistake. Although they didn't share a common language, Michael
nonetheless made them understand that he wanted them to stop, and
when they pulled over, he got out of the car.

Shortly thereafter, a caravan of Toyota test vehicles pulled up.
Death Valley issues special use permits to car makers to do heat testing
on the roads that go through the national park. Seeing the commotion
by the side of the road—Michael was still having trouble making
himself understood and had started shouting—the Toyota guys
stopped to help. They somehow let the tourists know they would take
care of Michael, and the tourists left. Michael got in a car with two of
the Toyota guys, and the rest left in the other three test vehicles. One
of them took Michael's backpack with the tracker in it, most likely by
mistake.

At that point, even if his cell phone could have caught a signal, he was in no shape to use it to call for help. Even as these men covered him with a wet towel and tried to give him water, he ranted that people were attempting to "kidnap" him. He tried to send them away, threatening to throw rocks at them and yelling. He succeeded in scaring them off, and they left him alone by the side of the road then drove six miles back to the Badwater basin parking area to call for help.

As soon as the National Park Service received their call, they dispatched an ambulance and called for a Mercy Air rescue flight from Las Vegas. By the time the Toyota test drivers made the call and the six-mile drive back to where they had left Michael alone, they found him lying well off the side of the road; he had turned and headed back into the desert, taken his shirt off, and fallen unconscious. Michael was frothing at the mouth, but they started CPR anyway. The men were able to flag down a van and convince the drivers to go off-road to put Michael in their vehicle (this was the third car Michael had been in since "finishing" his run), where they kept pumping his chest, trying to revive him. When the paramedics arrived and transferred Michael to their ambulance, they still continued CPR. The Mercy Air paramedics arrived and worked on Michael, too, to no avail.

It was a horrific ordeal for everyone involved—for those who tried and failed to rescue Michael, and for Sarah, especially, who arrived in time to see him in the back of the ambulance, blood spattering his oxygen mask during his final breaths. No doubt Michael suffered the most, from the initial headache and extreme thirst that morphed quickly into dizziness and nausea, then irritability and irrationality, and ultimately complete loss of his faculties. After Ben Jones performed the autopsy, he concluded that cause of death was "Heat-related, including asphyxiation due to pulmonary hemorrhaging."

Michael had departed from Sarah at 2:06 p.m., run 5.68 miles in under two hours, and arrived at Badwater Road at 3:56. From there, he'd been driven four miles south and gotten out of the tourists' vehicle around 4:03 p.m. The Toyota test drivers had arrived, gotten Michael into a vehicle, and tried to help him for about twenty minutes, left him, and returned to him probably at about 5:00 p.m. Michael was pronounced dead at 5:55 p.m. despite the efforts of more than ten people, including emergency responders.[6]

I heard about the tragedy from Denise Jones when Heather called from the ranger station just outside of Lone Pine to tell our friends that Dave and I had made it. The timing was chilling. Michael had set off on his run about five hours after Dave and I finished our sixteen-day expedition, and he'd died less than four hours after that. I'm not a religious person, but this phrase came to mind: "There but for the grace of God go I."

We returned home after a couple of days with the enormity of Michael's death eclipsing what Dave and I had accomplished. Of course, it felt good to have finished our circumnavigation, but it was even more important to have survived it. As details trickled in, Heather became a huge support for Sarah, and was able to piece together a timeline of Michael's demise, and we were shocked at how quickly things had gone wrong. It reminded me of a saying that mountaineers have about the sometimes fatal indifference of the natural world: *the mountains don't care,* and it is the same with the desert.

PART IV

WATER

DIVING DEEP

I go to nature to be soothed and healed,
and to have my senses put in order.
—John Burroughs, naturalist and essayist

8

COURAGE

IN 2012, my friend Dave Heckman and I made the 425-mile, sixteen-day trek around Death Valley National Park, officially the hottest place on earth and the driest zone in North America. Seven days into our arid heat-fest, Dave decided to check out an artesian spring he had read about while researching the Saline Valley. Such springs are quite rare in the middle of the desert, so he couldn't resist going for a dip. He stripped down, jumped in, and splashed around with unrestrained glee, the underground water cooling him off and refreshing his dry, sand-battered body. He returned to camp dripping wet and swinging his hair, cheerfully pronouncing his brief plunge "unbelievable."

Despite Dave's memorable impression of Bo Derek, I wasn't enticed to walk down to the nearby pool. It was about 120°F that day, on par with the previous week's temperatures, but I didn't feel like I wanted a dunk. Truth is, I'm not drawn to water, even under extreme circumstances like this. I fully understand that rivers, oceans, and lakes make for beautiful, serene landscapes, and just looking at a painting or photograph of any body of water soothes and calms the human mind. Scientific studies of this effect show that individuals viewing water images not only feel good but extend their attention spans, too, leading researchers to conclude that such images provide a "mental rest period."[1] And, sure, I enjoy a beautiful view of the water, or camping by a stream and letting the sounds of it lull me to sleep at night, but generally I'm more in my element when I'm tromping around in the desert or climbing a mountain than going for a dip.

Some people love water, some don't, and many are ambivalent. In her blog, world-class ocean rower Roz Savage confessed, "I love it, hate it, fear it, respect it, resent it, cherish it, loathe it, and frequently curse it. It brings out the best in me—and sometimes the worst."[2]

Her sentiments echo my feelings about nature itself, that when you immerse yourself in any wild environment, the experience isn't all butterflies and rainbows; sometimes it's leeches and windstorms. Ultimately, "getting back to nature" is a paradox filled with moments of both awe and *ah!*, feeling both connected and distinct, expansive and small, blithe yet profoundly moved. It's calming and dangerous, simple and complex, all at the same time, yet I am unequivocal in my endorsement: for me, time outside is crucial to my mental and physical health. It helps me sort out my thoughts and feelings or, if I go long enough, escape them. It lets me leave behind and burn away the pressures of business and the other demands of day-to-day busy-ness. I'm happiest in natural settings, surrounded by sand- and wind-sculpted geologic formations instead of human-made structures and the concomitant, incessant pinging and ringing of so many useful but annoying devices.

In contrasting the states of mind we experience in stressful environments—like working in an office building—with those we experience in relaxed environments—like vacationing at a lakeside retreat— marine biologist Wallace J. Nichols refers to that edgy, angry, and anxious state as "red mind," and the more relaxed state as "blue mind." The hormones present in red mind, he says, are a cocktail of norepinephrine, dopamine, and cortisol—all stress responses we've evolved to protect ourselves in moments of danger. The same neuro-chemicals that gave our ancestors the surge in physical strength or speed to get away from a hungry tiger give modern humans a burst of agitated power, which can be useful if you are actually confronted with a wild animal while you're hiking, but are taxing and unhealthy when it's constantly triggered by more mundane stressors, like meetings and imminent deadlines, urgent text messages and email, or pending bills.

For many people, the red mind stress response is their baseline, and blue mind moments arise only rarely. Nichols writes about the dangers of mistakenly feeling as if we're in danger all the time: "Repeated and sustained stress can wreak havoc from head to toe. In fact, the top ten causes of death around the world can either be caused or exacerbated by stress.... Increased stress can affect our ability to learn, retain information, or create new memories. ... [It can leave] you feeling flat, exhausted, and depressed," and it can even kill you.[3]

There's no question that urban settings fire up the red mind and distract us from opportunities to experience blue mind. Being in nature isn't always tranquil and relaxing; to the contrary, it will inevitably spark moments of red mind, but the ratio gets reversed: the baseline can become blue mind, while the red mind moments become little shots of excitement and, in some cases, exhilaration.

For me, somewhat ironically, most of my red-mind moments in nature have come when I've been confronted with water. The sport of adventure racing, in particular, made me confront my fear of drowning, and forced me to gain some skill as a swimmer. More accurately, it gave me a sense of confidence in my teammates. Every adventure race involves skill in several endurance disciplines in multiple environs over several days—these are the sport's defining characteristics—and you can always count on these races to require at least one type of water-sport (e.g., kayaking or canoeing), some kind of cross-country slog (running or trekking), mountain biking, and a wild card or two (camel riding, canyoneering, you name it). Success depends on solid navigation, orienteering, athleticism, and teamwork.

My love for the sport began when Chuck Blish, a fellow Coloradan, invited me to join his Team Mile High, and I signed on after talking with him for about twenty minutes on the phone. It was clear this would be a chance to expand my athletic skills, challenge my mental prowess, help me keep my love of running fresh with new experiences, and join a team where each of us would draw strength from the others. The race he proposed that I enter with him, the 1995 Eco-Challenge in Utah[4], would also be the first adventure race in North America.

Chuck told me he was putting together a group of athletes with skills in various parts of the course, and he thought I'd be a great addition, not only because of my experience and success with off-road running, but because I had a rep as being something of a glutton for punishment. He sensed that nothing would make me give up, no matter how tough things got. He mentioned that we'd be doing some river rafting and that we'd be dealing with some Class V rapids (which meant nothing to me at the time), but there were others on the team who'd take the lead on the river. He explained, nonchalantly, "It's big water, but with any luck, we'll get through it."

Team Mile High included our captain, Chuck, who was an expert rock climber and mountain biker; Justin Bein, a Special Forces Army man with survival skills who would serve as our navigator; Daphne Solone, a triathlete; and Mark ("Mace") Macy and me, both ultrarunners. Mace and I had known each other for a few years, and I'd admired his accomplishments at the Leadville hundred-mile trail races and during Ironman competitions (he started doing those waaaaaay before it was fashionable, and he was always with the leaders coming out of the water in the swimming phase). We seemed to have all the bases covered, and before we left for the Eco-Challenge, the team trained together a few times. All of us but Mace spent hours on the Colorado River learning to raft and practicing extreme fastpacking in the foothills of Colorado. All five of us traveled to Moab, Utah to learn the ropes and climb rock faces. We also got together in our local area, and we did our best to figure out what skills we'd need, muddled through in our own "special" ways, and spent a lot of time laughing at ourselves, which was perhaps the most important skill we learned before we arrived at the race.

Like me, Mace also had the reputation for persisting no matter what, and that was put to the test in the first few days of the Eco-Challenge. We spent the first seventy-two hours in Utah wading, swimming, and scrambling through rivers and cold slot canyons, often a bit confused and out of water to drink while we were in the high desert. Our packs and equipment were too heavy, navigational skills inept, climbing not to be admired, and whitewater skills crude, to put it kindly.

We were clearly overmatched. As Chuck had said, the course included Class V ("Expert") rapids in Canyonlands National Park, and

I suddenly, fully, appreciated what this means: the whitewater had been rated as appropriate for people who are capable of managing violent rapids and drops with "large, unavoidable waves and holes or steep, congested chutes with complex, demanding routes."[5] In short, it was big, big water, and I was in over my head, figuratively if not literally. What Chuck should have said was that we'd need a helluva lot more than luck to get through it.

Thank goodness the race directors provided an expert guide to take us through Cataract Canyon, part of the Colorado River. Something like 90 percent of the teams overturned in the rapids, but we shot through unscathed, paddling like hell and scared shitless with Mace in the front of the boat. We'd lied to him, saying the front was the best place to be, and he'd fallen for it since he'd never been rafting before, and Chuck hadn't given him even the scraps of info he'd given me. We'd joked that Mace would be our sacrifice to the water gods, that we'd all be in danger, but he'd have the best seat in the house. As we shot the rapids, Mace's eyes widened and he started spewing profanities as profusely as the river spewed water on us. Afterward, we all laughed—that nervous laugh people share when they come out unscathed from an especially harrowing ordeal—and acknowledged that we'd all been scared like we'd never been scared before.

These class V rapids we had to raft during the 1995 Eco-Challenge in Utah.

We enjoyed a few shining moments on land, as well. On day three, we approached Capital Reef and had to decide which canyon to go down. Trying to hone our navigation "skills," Mace stood on the edge of one canyon, and I on another, and we yelled to each other.

"Do you see anything?"

"No! Do you see anything?"

"No!"

So we made a blind decision, and we chose the wrong canyon. When we reached the bottom of Capital Reef hours later, Chuck, Justin, and Daphne made their own decision: they were withdrawing from the race. Looking despondent, they conceded that they'd had enough.

Our team was officially disqualified then, but Mace and I realized that we didn't much care about our race status; we were having the time of our lives. We continued for a dozen miles or so to reach the correct canyon, where we met the remaining members of another team, Columbia Sport: Robert (Dr. Bob) Haugh, Lisa Smith-Batchen, and Cory Shane. We decided to band together and dubbed ourselves "Team Columbia High."

The five of us finished the first Eco-Challenge as a fragmented, unofficial team, and I came away with true respect for the sport. I learned that having a good time was instrumental to finishing. The 370-mile race was a process, just like life, with inevitable ups and downs. Taking things in stride, and looking at every problem as something to be solved, rather than something to complain about, was the key to not letting anything or anyone beat us down. I realized that living life to its fullest was the ticket to finding out more about myself. I had touched upon this within the solitude of ultrarunning, but this was different: I wasn't alone, I was part of a team, and we could look to each other and draw strength, growing stronger together and as individuals. Just as important, adventure racing afforded us a chance to take a good look at our weaknesses. It allowed us to identify those weaknesses—the ones that could cripple us in a race, or in life—and try to grow beyond them.

Shortly after we finished the Eco-Challenge in Utah, Mace, Dr. Bob, Lisa, and I joked about how we'd come from all over the country and then wandered around the course like a bunch of stray dogs. We decided that was a great team name and determined to compete together again. After that, people would often ask why we called ourselves Team Stray Dogs and, depending on the company, we might joke, "We're just four mutts and a bitch."

Over the next decade, we continued to race together and developed a deep bond and admiration for one another. I can't tell you how many times Mace saved my ass, at least once tying a tow line around me to get me through a particularly long swim. Lisa was game for and good at just about any athletic test you could throw at her, and laughed her way through most of it. Dr. Bob always took everything in stride and, I swear, nothing fazed him. I've never heard him cuss once—which can't be said of any of the rest of us (Mace and I are the worst offenders)—and he was always the soul of calm and the opposite of complaint. They are some truly remarkable people.

In *Runner's World Guide to Adventure Racing,* Ian Adamson writes, "You lose brain cells each time you race. Thanks to those lost brain cells, a type of amnesia sets in after each race, allowing you to forget how much you suffered. The more races you compete in, the more brain cells you lose, until each race melds into the next. At this point, your life becomes adventure racing. If you have any interests outside the sport, you should give them up right now or go and hit your head repeatedly with a large hammer until you forget about them."

No doubt I've lost a few brain cells to sleep deprivation during adventure racing, just as Ian suggests, and I can attest to the lure of the sport. After that first Eco-Challenge, I was hooked, and I raced at least once a year for nine years (1995–2003).[6] The teams I was on produced respectable results, sometimes finishing in the top ten and as high as second. Team Stray Dogs reunited a few times, often with one or two new members substituting for anyone who couldn't make the trip. As a result, I had the good fortune to race with many stellar athletes, including Adrian Crane, Angelika (Drake) Castaneda, Rebecca Rusch, and Mike Kloser. You can see footage from some of those events online, as they were filmed for MTV, ESPN, the USA Network, and the Discovery Channel, which won an Emmy for the broadcast. Search online for the names of my teammates, and you'll find some impressive stats from their individual athletic careers, too.

Of course, every one of the adventure races had the dreaded water element. In British Columbia, we plunged into a glacial river, which swept me downstream a couple of hundred yards before one of the safety personnel plucked me out like a fish on a string; he hauled me to the opposite bank, where I lay flopping around until I could rid myself of leg cramps. In Australia, we faced ten-foot waves rolling along the reef as we entered the ocean in sea kayaks, only to be the last ones called off the course on account of the building storm. (We sheltered for a time on a nearby island not far from the finish line.)

In Morocco, it was fifteen-foot waves and over fifty-mile-per-hour winds, some of the roughest water I've ever experienced.

The deceptively calm start of the sea kayaking leg of the 1998 co-Challenge in Morocco.

During that race, too, we ran out of water and trekked for a day and a half in the Sahara Desert without it—only to have a man appear, some kind of desert genie, on his way to a well and then help us out by filling our water bottles. As suddenly as he had arrived, he disappeared over the horizon, and the desert was empty save our team. In Argentina, we paddled across serene lakes and portaged over rough land. In complete contrast, a rogue wave hit our outrigger in the South China Sea, capsizing us in the first hour of the race. Through laughter and sheer force of will, we surprised ourselves and everyone else by righting the craft and carrying on.

In 2002, we headed to Fiji, where Mark Burnett said that this would be the toughest Eco-Challenge ever, and he even offered money back, "no questions asked," to any team that decided at the last minute that they didn't want to do it. He predicted that, because of the difficulty of the course, only a few teams would be able to finish, and he announced there would be a swimming benchmark as a safety measure.

To qualify for the race, competitors had to swim four laps in a hundred-meter pool in a certain amount of time. I simply couldn't do it, even after a few tries. When I couldn't swim the distance in the required time, Mark was incredulous. He turned to Mace and asked him, "Why didn't you tell me Marshall can't swim?"

Mace gave Mark a matter-of-fact look and stated with no uncertainty, "Listen, don't be so horrified. If you threw Marshall into the middle of the ocean with a hundred other people, he'd be the only one to wash ashore alive." Mace had complete confidence in my tenacity and will to live, thinking they'd overcome even my terrible swimming skills. I guess Mark thought he was right, because he tried to figure out another way to qualify me for the race.

Or maybe he wanted to believe it, because it would have been an embarrassment to the Eco-Challenge if our team had been disqualified under this rule; I'd already competed so often that it would look bad. So Burnett decided to devise a special test for me and a few others who had failed in the pool: we went to the beach, where he'd placed a buoy about a half mile out, and he gave us flippers and instructions to swim to the buoy and back. No time limit. That, I could do, and our team was qualified to race.

Around midnight, we were loaded on a bus and driven to the start in the middle of a field. For two cold, overcast days we swam canyons and trekked up streams because the jungle was too dense to travel through. And, as with every Eco-Challenge, after a couple of days the difficulty of the race reduced everyone's egos. In this race, by the end of the second day, just as Mark had predicted, half the teams missed the first cutoff.

The second night, we decided it was too dangerous to travel

through giant boulders in the dark, so we stopped and huddled beside a stream. Our teammate Dianette Strange, who has almost no body fat, became hypothermic. As Dianette shivered uncontrollably, we took turns huddling and trying to keep her warm. At times she would slip into a barely conscious state and speak incoherently. It was a long, fearful night, and we were thankful when dawn broke, enabling us to move and generate the precious energy that is a key to staying warm.

The next four days continued to be cold and overcast as we paddled up streams, trekked up even more streams, and mountain biked up and down obscure trails and muddy dirt roads—and we watched still more teams drop out. Finally, we crossed over to the opposite side of the island and were bathed in sunshine. At last, warmth! On the seventh day, we finally reached our gear boxes and could change our clothes and get more food.

On our tenth and last day, we rappelled down a cliff near a stream. As I hopped onto a boulder eight feet above the stream bed, my feet slipped out from under me, and I found myself falling head first. Next thing I knew, I was lying in the stream bed, reaching into my mouth to see if I had lost any teeth or broken my jaw. Luckily, my water bottle, which was on my backpack shoulder strap next to my chin, had absorbed the impact, saving my jaw, and although my right shoulder ached, I was mostly intact.

Mace came running up and asked if I was okay. When I said yes, he shifted gears, smirking at me. He joked that as he'd watched me fall, his first thought had been that it would be a bitch to get me out of there, and his second thought was that it would be a bummer to be out of the race so close to the finish. He gave me his hand, I got up, and we carried on, cursing and laughing.

We arrived at the ocean shore, where we hopped in the kayaks and paddled the short course to the finish. Burnett was right. Out of eighty-one teams that started the race, only twenty-three finished, and we were happy to be seventeenth.

———

ADVENTURE RACING PRESENTS opportunities to learn new technical skills and, more importantly, to learn about yourself and the importance of working with a great team. The Fiji Eco-Challenge was the last one of its kind, though I was fortunate to compete in other adventure races after that. Still, the Eco-Challenges and Raid Gauloises remain the gold standard as far as I'm concerned. Each of the nine Eco-Challenges I've participated in provided or reinforced valuable life lessons, particularly the necessity of humility, the treasure of true friendship, and the efficacy of humor as the antidote to misery. In addition, they gave me exciting opportunities to travel, to immerse myself into extraordinary geographical settings, to experience many different cultures, and to meet unique people.

Recently, I learned that Mark Burnett is resurrecting the Eco-Challenge, which will be in September 2019. The Stray Dogs have applied, and hope to be selected to compete. Don't you think that a badass geezer squad would make the contest that much more interesting? I look forward to the challenge, to the teamwork, to the laughs, and even the prospect of confronting and overcoming my fear of the water yet again.

9

REDEMPTION

WATER OFTEN SYMBOLIZES emotions and the subconscious, so it may be meaningful that, for most of my life, I've been hesitant about anything to do with it. I'm a poor swimmer, and it has taken many years and a lot of help from friends to gain a degree of comfort in the water. Similarly, it wasn't until my late forties and my romance with Heather, now my wife, that I marshaled the courage to dive into my past, to reconcile difficult feelings and actions.

Developing my first book, *Running on Empty*, was hard not only because I was dredging up the often painful realities of running thousands of miles, but also because I was examining my life: my childhood and the death of my first wife, Jean, my motivations and decisions after that, and my struggles as a husband and father. Telling the story honestly was important to me, and I didn't want to portray myself as superhuman or as some kind of hero without faults; I'm as human as they come.

In his foreword to that book, Chris McDougall theorized that my single-mindedness during extreme tests of endurance had come from a refusal to look back, to examine where I'd been. Perhaps he's right. During that time in my life, my grief and pain over personal tragedies kept my eyes focused strictly on the road ahead. And he may have been right about something else, too: the turning point for me came as I wrote that book, not just recounting a single adventure, but piecing together a larger story with Heather's help. Doing that forced me to be introspective, to reflect on all that I'd done, considering both my successes and failures, as well as those things that I'd never assessed at all.

The crucial factor in my willingness to do that, then and now, was and is Heather's influence. As we begin to grow old together, we continue what began in the early, falling-in-love stages of our relationship: an honest examination of what's really important, what's true for us, what's best right now. Years ago, I spent a couple of hours a day training, conditioning my body for extreme tests of endurance. Back then, I ran faster and farther. Now, my priorities have shifted, and I am striving for greater success in my family life as a husband, father, and grandfather. This means letting go of some of the ambitiousness of my youth, and I need to do it. I have to do it. I want to do it.

Yet in some ways I am who I have always been: a farmer and an athlete, a dreamer with both feet on the ground, literally and figuratively. Heather's greatest gift to me has been loving all of me (and not just the parts that she agrees with or that make her comfortable). One of my defining characteristics is my deep affinity for the natural world with its paradoxical beauty and harshness. Each new experience outdoors reminds me of all the other times I spent learning about and exploring what Mother Earth has to offer, which sometimes included risk.

Nature compels me to sit on the back deck and listen to the sounds outside, the rustling of the trees, the singing of the birds, feeling the bite of the cold or the heat of the day. Adventure has sharpened my senses and allowed them to develop an acute awareness. It slows my breath, stills my heart, and calms my soul when I relax into it, feeling that I'm a part of it, that we are all a part of it. It causes me to reflect on those precious people in my life, amplifying how much they matter to me and drawing my attention to their individual personalities. In thinking of them, my mind ranges over them much like the mountains in my memory, too, each alike but unique. A few examples of the power of nature follow.

ONE YEAR, I was about seventy miles into the 100-mile snowshoe race called the Iditafoot in Alaska. Long after dark, I was crossing the frozen Susitna River, and the Northern Lights were putting on an amazing show: greens, reds, and oranges danced across the midnight sky. I stopped, lay down on the ice, and marveled at the sight. It was a rare instance of calm connectedness, made even more unusual for me because of its association with the water, turned solid to hold me up. It was as if I could reach out, sweep my hand across the colors, and paint the heavens. All of my senses were attuned: the support of six feet of ice under my back, the boundless silence, the vivid display. Despite the ten-below temperature, it warmed my soul, and I must have stayed there for ten minutes, at least, though I'm not sure how long it was, because time ceased to exist for me. When I stood up at last, I felt refreshed, replenished, renewed, ready to move on. I was filled with joy and gratitude.

IN 1999, the year I succeeded in running the 146-mile Badwater Race course solo and self-contained, pulling all my supplies—most important, the life-giving water I needed to survive Death Valley's heat—I competed just a few weeks later in the Leadville Trail 100 ultramarathon and the Leadville Trail 100 Bike Race. On the bike, I came in dead last. In the run, I didn't perform as well as I'd hoped, either.

Feeling unsatisfied with this, feeling as if I had something to prove, I started looking for another event. (ow, looking back, I can see how unnecessary such "proof" was, but that was B.H., before Heather. My legs were t-i-r-e-d, but I was looking for something else I could do that would call on different reserves of strength. Always striving to complete the most creative challenge, to establish some innovative first, I remembered that a friend of mine had thought up a Leadville Triple: completing the bike, run, and then a hundred-mile kayak around nearby Turquoise Lake by circling it ten times. So I called Buzz Burell and asked if I could take his idea and run (paddle) with it. He said sure, as he didn't think he'd ever get around to doing it himself, and he thought it would be a fine test of endurance.

What I set out to do, then, was about redemption. As I dropped my kayak into the forty-five-or-so-degree water that day, I knew I had to do it. It rained some during the day and that night as I hugged the shore just in case I capsized. Uncomfortable the whole time, especially at night when I was at risk of falling asleep after more than twenty hours on the water, I fought through it. Air temps were near freezing. My gloved hands were so cold they were numb, and I sank them into the water to warm them up over and over again.

Yet there were moments of strangely calming solitude, like when the moon first popped out that night, and I felt alone—afraid, too, but at peace.

During the last part of my 1999 Leadville trip crown, a 100-mile paddle, I found calming solitude on Turquoise Lake.

And when I finished, more than twenty-eight hours later, I did feel redeemed. I had learned to reconcile my discomfort with a deep sense of serenity I had not found elsewhere that summer, neither pounding my feet nor pedaling my bike.

Not long ago, I posted an article on social media about this, a throwback to this little-known Leadville Triple. No one remembered that I'd done it, and I found that gratifying. Back in the day, no one publicized this sort of thing. I had done this quietly, under the radar, and for myself.

I believe you derive something powerful from failing and coming back stronger. Looking at the benefits of not always finishing what I start the first time, and making sure that I complete what I've started, has shaped me in unexpected ways, ways that have yielded some wisdom. I have failed in some things, and I have redeemed myself in most things. Revisiting challenges strengthens my fortitude and allows me to be confident that eventually I will be successful.

As my daughter Elaine told me before I ran across the U.S., "You will likely finish, but it may be a different experience or outcome than you expect." Was she ever right! That endeavor was longer, slower, and more difficult than I could ever have imagined. And sometimes the importance of whatever I have been trying to accomplish comes into sharper focus; sometimes, it simply isn't as important as I had originally thought. That, too, is a kind of success, an important lesson.

There is always a reckoning down the road—or stream, or mountain, or any other metaphorical or real elsewhere—and how we choose to deal with our successes or failures stays with us. There's no denying that, and in the long run, we have to be comfortable in our own skin. Being persistent and not letting anything stop you is vital—neither something (such as the weather, terrain, or some element that is out of my control) nor someone (telling me what I can or can't do or, worse yet, talking myself out of success)—but it takes practice and often trials and errors. We are all more resilient than we think, but don't often challenge ourselves to prove it. Look at it this way: Being unable to accomplish what we set out to do is just another chance to rise to the occasion, to prove that we are and always will be the strong, flexible, persistent person we hoped we were.

It's true that some things never change: I have found that proving myself remains vital to my psyche as I age, but my expectations and focus have to be continuously re-evaluated and adjusted. I still crave outdoor adventures and challenges, but I have different kinds of goals, such as spending more time with Heather or my grandchildren instead of beating around in the desert or trying to overcome fears of water or heights. Some stuff, I concede now, I do not have to prove anymore— not to my family, not to myself, and certainly not to anyone else.

That means, too, that some of my once-proudest accomplishments have become secondary. Now, it's not the athletic feats that matter so much, but what I've done my best to learn from them. When I meet people who have followed my career or read what I've written, I appreciate that they invested the time to get to know something about me, but the only thing that matters, really, is if that person has been inspired to do more than they thought they could. Helping people make positive changes is the work that, in some small way, maybe, changes the world. I hope that by revealing how difficult it has been for me to look within—but also how incredibly meaningful—I can move someone to this kind of action, too. Every day, especially every day outside in nature, is another chance at redemption.

10

REFLECTION

AS THE KEYNOTE speaker at a major financial organization's annual meeting, I talked about three of my most extreme events: climbing Mount Everest, which was the most technical; trekking the perimeter of Death Valley, which was the most dangerous; and running across America, which was the most difficult. In sharing that last one, I recalled how a doctor had told me that completing those 3,063 miles on foot had likely shortened my life by a few years. But, I told them, I didn't give a damn about that, as I had squeezed plenty out of my time here on earth. To my surprise, a handful of people jumped to their feet and cheered, and then the rest of the crowd went wild with applause, too.

It was much different from what happened after I finished addressing a group of seniors one afternoon, when a gentleman stood up during the question-and-answer session. We were on a cruise ship where I'd been booked as a speaker to help entertain the guests, and the crowd was different from the young athletes I usually meet, who are inclined either to act impressed with me (like the financial folks) or to tell me they're going to break my records. This crowd was older, accomplished, and affluent, with nothing to prove and generally bemused by some of the choices I'd made, particularly those that had put my life at stake for sport. The man who wanted to ask me a question was tall, distinguished-looking, probably in his mid-seventies, with a full head of silver hair and bright blue eyes. He was frowning a bit and took a moment to collect his thoughts. He sighed, and then he started talking.

"Your exploits are all well and good," he began, "but what about someone like me? I used to be able to do all sorts of things. I never climbed Mount Everest, but I did run marathons and went on safari once in Africa. Now that I'm older, I can't do that sort of thing anymore. What kind of message are you trying to give me, someone who couldn't do and probably *wouldn't want to do* what you have, even when I was at my peak?"

His question made me think, although part of it was easy to answer. "Don't compare yourself to me or anyone else, but do get outside and challenge yourself," I told him. "I agree, some of my exploits would be over the top for lots of people. Not everyone should do what I've done. Still, I am sure that anyone can have meaningful, inspiring adventures, regardless of the scale and in spite of age. For some people, that means tending a garden. Some may enter a triathlon. Some will lead weekly hikes. A few will climb mountains or run across deserts or paddle in the darkest jungles, like I have done, but it's not for me to say who should do what; only you know what's right for you. The key is to feel passionate about it and keep the juices flowing."

That much was familiar ground for me, as I'm encouraging people in this way all the time. The other part wasn't so simple. How does aging affect aspirations? How should it? Is there an expiration date on adventure? Growing older has brought me some disappointments, just as it had for this man. Since I entered my fifties, I don't run as fast as I used to, and it becomes more noticeable as I continue to age. From time to time, I wrestle with my expectations and my unpredictable ability to meet them, but then I remind myself that it is all relative and refocus on what I *can* do. In truth, I've always had to adjust and adapt or risk failing altogether. When I was fifty-seven and attempting to set a record by running across America, I had to talk myself out of a serious funk over having covered "only" fifty-five miles one day in Nebraska. In my mind, that was not good enough.

I'd been running every single day since leaving San Francisco—more than a thousand miles total and on average more than sixty miles a day—but I'd expected to do better. I'd fallen short, and I was beating myself up about it. Instead of staying in that state of self-pity and ornery disappointment, though, I made myself take stock and set a new goal.

That may seem to be a ridiculous example, being upset at covering fifty-five miles on foot in a day, but it perfectly illustrates my point. My disappointments aren't the same as yours, just as my aspirations aren't the same as yours. Maybe my athletic goals are more ambitious; maybe your goals are out of reach for me. Either way, it doesn't really matter.

It reminds me of that meme with two dogs, the golden retriever and the terrier, and the caption, "How deep is the mud?" The little dog is dirty up to the neck, while the bigger one is covered only up to the ankles. "Depends on who you ask," it says. Right! How deep is a matter of perspective, which doesn't mean the terrier isn't just as fine a dog as the retriever. Nor does it mean they shouldn't both get into the mud.

But with advancing age, should we temper our enthusiasm for adventure or just press on? This is what I wish I had told the man: "Perspective is a powerful calibrator. You can compare yourself to other people and wind up feeling inadequate and depressed, or you can do the same thing and feel inspired. *Look at what so-and-so does!* Then you can take it to the next level by aspiring to something all your own: *What can I do?* It's the same with our own pasts: we can compare our abilities today with what we once could do and be devastated by what we perceive as decline, or we can be grateful for what we have done and let that propel us to do something inspiring today.

I'd never suggest resting on your laurels, but I freely endorse another cliché: enjoying the fruits of your labor—and using them to fuel your next endeavor. Meaningful pursuits are rooted in reflection upon the ups and downs. Lessons from the mountaintops helped me go on in the lowest valleys, and vice versa. Challenges met and mastered informed how to deal with obstacles that not only seemed insurmountable but were, ultimately, too much for me to overcome. Each success bred self-reliance and self-regard, aspirations, discipline, and perseverance. Defeats provided an outlook that would have been less accessible from the vantage point of victory: humility, compassion, ingenuity, insight.

It's important for me to emphasize that I'm not only a guy who gets to the top of Mount Everest; I'm also a guy who fails, frequently. Some of my most heartbreaking setbacks have been personal ones, those that affected not only me but people I love. I've been married four times and divorced twice. I've struggled in my relationships with all three of my children. I've dealt with drama within both my immediate and extended family. And lest you think I'm some kind of superman in sports, you should know that I have failed in athletic tests, as well. I have been running for four decades and covered nearly a hundred thousand miles, and in that time and over that distance, I've dropped out of plenty of races, unable to finish. I once quit a seventy-two-hour race because I was physically and mentally ill-equipped for it, and I left with my tail between my legs, feeling embarrassed, my vanity pricking my pride. Recently, I was in a 240-mile race across the Gobi desert and messed up a critical calculation, causing me to miss the final cutoff time just twenty miles from the finish.

In 1998, the first time I attempted to do a self-contained solo on the Badwater course (146 miles across Death Valley and up Mount Whitney), I couldn't do it. As I detailed earlier, in 2012, when a friend and I trekked around the 425-mile perimeter of Death Valley, I nearly died in the desert heat because I hadn't planned to carry enough water one day, something I should have known better. There are many more examples like this. I screw up and I fall short all the time, just like everyone else. Just this summer, I failed at the Badwater course again, my fifth time earning a DNF ("did not finish") in that race. However, I have been successful twenty times; so, a week after dropping out, I returned to the course with my wife and a baby jogger filled with water, food, and supplies, which allowed me to run portions of the course by myself, while I enjoyed her company and care during most of the desert portion. After getting a permit, I climbed the mountain alone, finishing the entire 146 miles from Badwater Basin to the peak of Mount Whitney one more time, making it my twenty-fourth time doing so—at the tender age of sixty-six.

Some people say there's no such thing as failure, but of course there is. If we recognize success, which is the achievement of what you set out to do, then we have to acknowledge its opposite. Yet I don't think of failure as a black mark on character. As Winston Churchill said, success is not final, and failure is not fatal. Failure is merely a fact, and we can choose to accept that fact gracefully and with an effort to learn something from it even if the benefits aren't immediately apparent. Failure can be a powerful teacher; I've certainly learned more from my failures than from my successes.

Truly, the only limitations are in your mind. I don't mean that you can grow fins just because you want to be a world-class swimmer, or that you'll sprout wings if you just wish for them hard enough; I mean that you need to pay attention to the lessons of failure, and guard against self-imposed limitations that arise only from fear—such as fear of failing again—and you need to acknowledge that it's a mind game.

It's like reading a river in whitewater rafting. From one vantage point, the rapids may look impassable, so the best thing to do is to get off the river and scout it from the banks. Then just pick a route and go down whichever way looks feasible to go. Maybe you shoot through it without a problem, scared to death but carried through by a lot of luck. Maybe you capsize and have to persevere until you can get the vessel put right again. It's about sorting out your reactions, avoiding knee-jerks, and instead making considered decisions about intelligent risks.

Growing older, I still look forward to more adventures, although they might not be as daring; I am more understanding of myself just as I am, of nature and what it has to offer. For instance, when my daughter Ali climbed Mount Whitney with me in July 2018, it was one of the most joyful and important things I've done.

I see myself humbly stepping into a role that others I've admired have held—people like Ted Corbett and Admas Belilgne—elders of extreme sports. So I will keep pushing myself physically (Ted ran multiday races well into his eighties, setting records and showing the way for other aging athletes), and I will share my enthusiasm for outdoor adventure with anyone who aspires to squeeze the most out of life at any age.

Sharing my love of nature with my daughter, Ali (r) atop Mount Whitney in 2018.

All of my time outdoors has pushed me, chastened me, shattered preconceptions, given me solace. It has, on occasion, saved me from desperation and isolation, providing both escape and deep connection. Getting outside and into nature has given me a way to connect with myself when the world is confusing and out of my control. It has given me quietude and time to reflect on what is important, and, in my later years, those hours are often preoccupied with thoughts of my wife, my children, and my grandchildren. No matter how complicated my life may be, getting outside rights the wrong, helping me to see new perspectives, reminding me that life is fragile and I am vulnerable, revealing my weaknesses and reassuring me of my strengths. The more I engage with the natural world, the more in tune I am with myself and the people around me. In a word, nature *grounds* me.

May it ground you, too. I hope you find excitement in the world outside, and peace, also. Let it enliven your imagination and lift your spirits. It can inspire you not only to take advantage of every adventure it has to offer but also to take care of it, to hold dear the beauty and magnitude of it. To that end, I leave you with this Ute prayer:

Earth teach me quiet, as the grasses are still with new light.
Earth teach me suffering, as old stones suffer with memory.

*Earth teach me humility, as blossoms are humble with
    beginning.*
Earth teach me caring, as mothers nurture their young.
Earth teach me courage, as the tree that stands alone.
Earth teach me limitation, as the ant that crawls on the ground.
Earth teach me freedom, as the eagle that soars in the sky.
Earth teach me acceptance, as the leaves that die each fall.
Earth teach me renewal, as the seed that rises in the spring.
Earth teach me to forget myself, as melted snow forgets its life.
*Earth teach me to remember kindness, as dry fields weep with
    rain.*

NOTES

Introduction

1. Louv, Richard. *Last Child in the Woods: Saving Our Children from Nature Deficit Disorder* (New York: Algonquin Books, 2008), p. 36.
2. Yates, Diana. "The science suggests access to nature is essential to human health," *News Bureau:* University of Illinois website (Feb. 13, 2009). http://www.news.illinois.edu/news/09/0213nature.htmlaccessed Jan. 14, 2015.

1. Grounding

1. Charlie Jordan, "Porter Captures Mt. Evans Trophy Run," Rocky Mountain Running News Sept. 1981 (4:8), p. 1.
2. "High Schoolers Don't Know Where Food Comes From," TakePart.com (Sept. 11, 2015). http://www.takepart.com/video/2015/09/11/high-schoolers-dont-know-where-food-comes
3. Burns, Judith. " 'Cheese is from plants' – study reveals child confusion," BBC.com (June 3, 2013). http://www.bbc.com/news/education-22730613
4. "Nationwide Surveys Reveal Disconnect Between Americans and their Food," PRNewswire.com (Sept. 22, 2011). http://www.prnewswire.com/news-releases/nationwide-surveys-reveal-disconnect-between-americans-and-their-food-130336143.html
5. Mack, Edward. "Study Proves Farm Dirt Is Beneficial for Children's Health," *Wide Open Country,* Sept. 29, 2015. http://www.wideopencountry.com/study-proves-farm-dirt-is-beneficial-for-childrens-health/ accessed 10/1/15.

2. Sustenance

1. Cary Funk and Lee Rainie, "Public and Scientists' Views on Science and Society," Pew Research Center. Accessed Nov. 15, 2015: http://www.pewinternet.org/2015/01/29/public-and-scientists-views-on-science-and-society/
2. "GMO Foods: What You Need to Know," *Consumer Reports* (Feb. 26, 2015). Accessed Nov. 19, 2015: http://www.consumerreports.org/cro/magazine/2015/02/gmo-foods-what-you-need-to-know/index.htm
3. Michael Pollan, *Food Rules* (New York: Penguin Books, 2009), pp. xii-xii.
4. "Protein," Harvard T. H. Chan School of Public Health website. Accessed Nov. 20, 2015: http://www.hsph.harvard.edu/nutritionsource/what-should-you-eat/protein/
5. "Protein," ibid.
6. Karin Kratina, PhD, RD, LD/N. "Orthorexia Nervosa," *NationalEatingDisorders.org.* https://www.nationaleatingdisorders.org/orthorexia-nervosa accessed Nov. 4, 2015.
7. David Zeevi, Tal Korem, Niv Zmora, et al. "Personalized Nutrition by Prediction

of Glycemic Responses," *Cell* (Vol. 163, Iss. 5, p. 1079—1094, Nov. 19, 2015). Accessed on Nov. 23, 2015: http://www.cell.com/cell/abstract/S0092-8674(15)01481-6

3. Daring

1. DuLong, Jessica. "Swallow Your Fear," *Psychology Today* (Nov. 1, 2006). https://www.psychologytoday.com/articles/200612/swallow-your-fear, accessed 2/27/15.

4. Acclimation

1. Gary Scott, *Summit Strategies* (Hillsboro, Oregon: Beyond Words Publishing, Inc., 2013), 67.
2. It was unchallenged except for a niggling controversy over whether Chad Kellogg —who had support at camps along the way from people who gave him water, food, clothing and other gear—could be considered to have broken the record in 2003. Everyone with a shred of expertise on the subject dismissed that claim. A supported climb over this many hours is vastly different from—*significantly easier than*—one completed without help. It's apples and oranges, my friends, or at least oranges and grapefruits. In 2014, however, Kilian Jornet set a new record for an unsupported climb, reaching the top in eleven hours and forty-eight minutes, although he used a shorter route and wore lightweight racing skis.
3. Gary Scott. Ibid. p. 70.
4. Gary Scott, email message to author, May 18, 2015.
5. Indeed, this was the same Charlie Engle who attempted to run across America with me years later in 2008. For more on that roller coaster, see my book *Running on Empty*.
6. Ruth Chang, "How to make hard choices." Accessed March 6, 2015. http://www.ted.com/talks/ruth_chang_how_to_make_hard_choices?language=en
7. James Hamblin, "Buy Experiences, Not Things," *The Atlantic,* Oct. 7, 2014. Accessed May 21, 2015. http://www.theatlantic.com/business/archive/2014/10/buy-experiences/381132/.
8. James R. McGoodwin, *Understanding the Cultures of Fishing Communities* (FAO Fisheries Technical Paper 401, Food & Agriculture Org., 2001): 184.

5. Altitude

1. "Chains, We Don't Need No Stinking Chains," *ExplorersWeb,* Jan. 18, 2004, http://www.mounteverest.net/story/stories/Chains,wedontneednostinkinchains-Jan182004.shtml, accessed July 16, 2015.
2. Rachel Nuwer, "The Tragic Tale of Mount Everest's Most Famous Dead Body," *BBC.com,* October 8, 2015. http://www.bbc.com/future/story/20151008-the-tragic-story-of-mt-everests-most-famous-dead-body accessed August 25, 2017.
3. Laura Parker, "Will Everest's Climbing Circus Slow Down After Disasters?" *National Geographic,* May 13, 2015. http://news.nationalgeographic.-

com/2015/05/150513-everest-climbing-nepal-earthquake-avalanche-sherpas/ accessed July 23, 2015.

4. Alan Arnette, "Everest 2015: The Cost to Climb Everest," *AlanArnette.com* blog, December 15, 2014. http://www.alanarnette.com/blog/2014/12/15/everest-2014-cost-climb-everest/ accessed July 23, 2015.

5. Justin Moyer, "Nepal's earthquake and why Mount Everest should be closed—permanently," *The Washington Post,* April 27, 2015. http://www.washingtonpost.com/news/morning-mix/wp/2015/04/27/why-mt-everest-should-be-closed-permanently/ accessed July 23, 2015.

6. Reinhold Messner, *Everest: Expedition to the Ultimate* (Sheffield, England: Vertebrate Digital), 2014.

7. Justin Moyer. Ibid.

8. Svati Kirsten Narula, "Charting Deaths on Mount Everest," *The Atlantic,* April 21, 2014. http://www.theatlantic.com/international/archive/2014/04/mortality-on-mount-everest/360927/ accessed July 23, 2015.

9. Paul Cronin, *Werner Herzog – A Guide for the Perplexed: Conversations with Paul Cronin* (London: Faber and Faber, 2014.)

6. Perseverance

1. Email from Stan's daughter to Chris Kostman dated Nov. 11, 2013.

2. Lee Green. "Defying Death Valley," *Spirit* (June 1994).

3. Bob Wischnia. "Al Arnold: The Road Goes on Forever," *Marathoner* (Spring 1978/Premiere Issue), http://www.badwater.com/wp-content/uploads/2014/07/arnoldmarathonermag1.pdf, accessed Feb. 16, 2016

4. Al Arnold. "The True Spirit of the Race," Badwater.com, http://www.badwater.com/blog/category/al-arnolds-insights/page/2/ accessed Jan. 27, 2016.

5. Greg Larson. "Jay Birmingham Sets Another Record, 1981," *Florida Times-Union* (Aug. 19, 1981), http://www.badwater.com/blog/jay-birmingham-sets-another-record-1981/ accessed Feb. 18, 2016.

6. Of some note: In addition to his race with Maxwell in 1970, Crutchlow had completed a relay across Death Valley in 1973, and returned for a rematch against Maxwell in 1976. (Maxwell again prevailed with a six-hour margin.) At the 1987 British v. Americans face-off, Crutchlow was forty-five years old and reported to have been fifteen pounds overweight.

7. Chris Kostman. "1987: The Year Badwater Became a Race," from *Runner's World* (August 1988), http://www.badwater.com/blog/1987-the-year-badwater-became-a-race/ accessed Feb. 18, 2016.

8. Email from Dave Pompel to Marshall Ulrich dated March 1, 2016.

9. Bart Yasso, "The Word According to Bart Yasso: The wit, wisdom, and globe-trotting adventures of a running icon," *Runner's World* (May 10, 2008). http://www.runnersworld.com/runners-stories/the-world-according-to-bart-yasso accessed Jan. 27, 2016.

10. Bart Yasso, Ibid.

7. Retreat

1. Shultz, Colin. "At 107°F, Death Valley Sets Record for Hottest Daily Low," *Smithsonian.com* (July 18, 2012). Accessed May 18, 2016, http://www.smithsonianmag.com/smart-news/at-107f-death-valley-sets-record-for-hottest-daily-low-3428045/
2. "National Overview – July 2012: July daily temperature extremes," National Centers for Environmental Information: National Oceanic and Atmospheric Administration website accessed May 18, 2016, https://www.ncdc.noaa.gov/sotc/national/2012/7/supplemental/page-7/
3. http://weathersource.com/account/official-weather?location=Death+Valley%2C+CA&start-date=07%2F22%2F2012&end-date=7%2F29%2F2012&subscription-demo=1&sid=bsibno4itu2s7akfq3ophcg882&search=1&station-id=25807&latitude=36.4256&longitude=-117.09
4. *Dreamland: Adventures in the Strange Science of Sleep* by David K. Randall and published by W. W. Norton & Company in 2012.
5. Gordon Wright, "Michael Popov's last run: Coming to grips with the sudden death of an exceptional ultrarunner," *Outside.com*, accessed June 15, 2016, http://www.outsideonline.com/1902996/michael-popov%E2%80%99s-last-run-coming-grips-sudden-death-exceptional-ultrarunner
6. My account differs from what you might read elsewhere, mainly because the early reporting of Michael's death had a number of inaccuracies. This version of events is based on information Heather gathered from the National Park Service and other official agencies, as well as conversations with Sarah Spelt and Ben Jones.

8. Courage

1. M. White, A. Smith, et al., "Blue space: the importance of water for preference, affect, and restorativeness ratings of natural and built scenes," *Journal of Environmental Psychology* 30 (2010), 482-93.
2. Savage, Roz. "The Ocean Rower's Perspective on Climate Change," RozSavage.com, 15 October 2009.
3. Wallace J. Nichols, *Blue Mind: The Surprising Science That Shows How Being Near, In, On, or Under Water Can make You Happier, Healthier, More Connected, and Better at What You Do*, p. 143-144
4. Organized by Mark Burnett—who has since produced the TV shows *Survivor, The Apprentice*, and *Shark Tank*, as well as the movies *The Bible* (2013) and *Ben-Hur* (2016)—the Eco-Challenge was modeled on the Raid Gauloises, a French multi-day race organized by Gerald Fusil, who had pioneered the sport in New Zealand. Reportedly, Mark collected numerous credit cards and, by design, forced himself deep into debt to pull together the debut in Utah.
5. International Scale of River Difficulty set by the American Whitewater association. http://www.americanwhitewater.org/content/Wiki/safety:start?#vi
6. Eco-Challenge Utah, 1995; ESPN Extreme Games/Eco-Challenge New England, 1995; Eco-Challenge British Columbia, 1996; Eco-Challenge Australia, 1997; Eco-Challenge Morocco, 1998; Eco-Challenge Argentina, 1999; Eco-Challenge Sabah, 2000; Eco-Challenge New Zealand, 2001; Eco-Challenge Fiji, 2002

ACKNOWLEDGMENTS

Many thanks to my wife Heather for believing in me and helping me to forge a unique path in this world. Her love is undying. To my children, Elaine, Taylor, and Ali who have experienced and seen my ups and downs their entire lives: thank you for your perseverance and support throughout all my adventures! I hope you, your spouses, and your children may find a bit of inspiration in my struggles, and my accomplishments.

To those who have helped and guided me through the process of writing this, my second, book: my agent Stephen Hanselman, his wife Julia Serebrinsky, and dear friends and extraordinary people Karen Risch Mott and Perry Gray. Thanks also to Megan Newman at Penguin/Avery who helped me kick off my writing career by editing my first book, *Running on Empty*.

I thank all of my friends who have shared running a mile or two, climbed a mountain, or experienced perilous disciplines all over the world during expedition-length adventure races. Especially Mark Macy, Dr. Bob Haugh, and Jill Andersen; you continue to be my dear and best friends, lifting me up when times are down.

Thanks to all of you who have thirsted for adventure and faced the challenges that nature can provide, discovering that peace of mind and calming of soul can indeed be found in the great and wild outdoors. Finally, thanks to all of you who may now find excitement in the world outside; may it refresh and ground you.

ABOUT THE AUTHOR

 Marshall Ulrich (b. July 4, 1951) is a farmer, used cow dealer, ultrarunner, Seven Summits mountaineer, adventure racer, explorer, speaker, and best-selling author. His first book, *Running on Empty*, used his record-setting run across America in 2008 as the thread to tie together some of the painful, funny, and life-changing lessons he's learned through his thirty-five years as an endurance athlete. In *Both Feet on the Ground*, he shares stories from adventures in racing, trekking, and mountaineering in places like Tibet, Fiji, and Death Valley. The most important lessons he's learned through these extreme adventures in nature are about senses that used to be common among people who lived closer to the land. Join him, and learn how to let the natural world ground you.

Learn more at MarshallUlrich.com.

ALSO BY MARSHALL ULRICH

Running on Empty:

An Ultramarathoner's Story of Love, Loss, and

a Record-Setting Run Across America

Made in the USA
Coppell, TX
10 May 2020

24267909R10105